You Are My God

By the same author

One in the Spirit
I Believe in Evangelism
I Believe in the Church
Study Guide to I Believe in the Church
Is Anyone There?
Discipleship
Fear No Evil

You Are My God

an autobiography
by

David Watson

HODDER AND STOUGHTON
LONDON SYDNEY AUCKLAND TORONTO

To all our Christian brothers and sisters in York who shared with us, both in joy and in pain, through the seventeen best years of our life.

British Library Cataloguing in Publication Data

Watson, David *1933–1984*
   You are my God : an autobiography
   1. Christian life
   I. Title
   248.4   BV4501.2

ISBN 0–340–39129–4

Contents

Acknowledgments

In attempting to write an honest account of my last twenty-eight years since I became a Christian, I have included a number of painful incidents, as well as referring to times of great joy and blessing. I am especially grateful to Anne, my wife, for her wise advice during the writing of this manuscript and for her patient acceptance of me over the years, without which this book could never have been written.

I have valued too the encouragements and suggestions of a number of friends who read the manuscript, in particular Edward England, my literary agent whose shrewd counsel I constantly treasure.

Most of all I want to thank Hilary Saunders, my secretary, both for her helpful comments during the exacting time of writing and for her untiring efforts with the typewriter.

Biblical quotations, unless otherwise stated, are from the Revised Standard Version.

Foreword

I knew David Watson many years before. As Archbishop of York, I encountered him again. He had been a curate in St. Mark's, Gillingham, when I was Warden of Rochester Theological College, and we had met several times. However, nothing in his past had prepared me for what I found at St. Michael-le-Belfrey here in the centre of York. It was a church destined for redundancy (as well it might be in a city which boasted nearly forty parish churches) which, within a few months of David's arrival, was attracting large congregations of young and old, and sending them out as enthusiasts for Christ and witnesses to him in the world. The services were of a kind which we now associate with the renewal movement: swinging music, warm fellowship and manifest signs of the Spirit. But what made St. Michael's so significant was that these now-familiar phenomena were under-girded by a consistent thorough programme of teaching undertaken, in the first instance, by David himself. Membership of the congregation was no easy option. It called for persistent attention to the word of God; it discouraged personal fantasies unrelated to everyday life, and it required from everyone some ministry to others, whether it was by way of personal testimony or extended families or drama or running a shop. It has been a huge enterprise, with ramifications all over the world. The 'renewal weeks' have been attended by priests and lay people from as far afield as the USA and Malta. It transcends the boundaries of race and denomination.

Of course, there have been difficulties and David Watson and his fellow ministers would be the last to gloss over them. But in the main it has been a triumph of grace, striking evidence that the Spirit of God is at work among us, and that the Kingdom is not just part of some unimaginable future, but a present reality in the lives of individuals and of groups. David, to me, is not just a highly successful parish priest, but a personal friend who stands for those things I value above all in the life of the Church and in its mission to the world. It is against this background that you need to read the book you now have in your hand. The title is perhaps typical of the man – you may well learn more of God than of David from this autobiography.

Stuart Ebor
Bishopthorpe, York
14th March 1983

Introduction

For years I have resisted the pressure to write about our experiences in York. The growth of a congregation from almost nothing to 700 or more can be overrated. Many other churches have moving stories to tell, and anyway both at St. Cuthbert's and St. Michael-le-Belfrey in York we had suffered in the past from too much exposure. Added to that, I knew that the apparent triumphalism of Christian 'success' stories could sometimes discourage those who were battling with ordinary problems. I was also acutely aware of the spiritual dangers of the 'cult of personality'. This is acceptable in the secular sphere of superstars, but it is divisive in the Christian Church. It was so at Corinth in New Testament days, and it is sadly the same in some Christian circles today.

The Christian Gospel is not about superstars, 'so let no one boast of men' wrote the apostle Paul (1 Cor. 3:21). It is rather about God's extraordinary grace in spite of very ordinary human faults and failings, and also his blessings in the midst of suffering. It is with these truths in mind that I have tried to write honestly about both the pain and the joy that we have experienced. Some of this relates specifically to my personal spiritual pilgrimage in different places and at different times; much of it refers to our corporate experiences as a congregation in York; but some of it deliberately speaks about our own marriage. Both Anne and I know that Christians have no immunity from the marriage problems that afflict society so widely today. For this reason we agreed that I should be open about the difficulties that we too have experienced, especially now that we have worked through these traumas to a more mature and strong relationship.

The glib message of 'Come to Christ and all will be well!', or 'Be filled with the Spirit and your problems will be solved!', finds no echo in the pages of the New Testament. Certainly God promises us the 'unsearchable riches of Christ', and the epistles are full of superlatives: love which surpasses knowledge, peace which passes all understanding, joy inexpressible . . . but interwoven with these are the darker threads of pain and tears, weakness and sin, suffering and strife. The astonishing Good News of Christ is that he loves us just as we are and can work through us just as we are. No human frailty needs be a hindrance to God's infinite grace.

It is obvious that I have had to be highly selective in choosing material, and this book may be more remarkable for what it does not say than for what it does. Where possible I have tried to avoid painful references to any individuals since these would not help anyone. My ultimate purpose is to give a personal testimony to the reality of God in the varied spectrum of human experience. If through the sunshine and storms something of the light of Christ is seen in greater glory, this book will not be in vain.

1

Experiment of Faith

'I'll see you there at four,' said Sam, reflecting my cynical grin, as we accepted yet another invitation.

Our little plan had been working well. As old school friends, Sam and I had just started at Cambridge University. Like every other first-year student, we had been urged to join every conceivable club, from tennis to tiddly-winks, fencing to philosophy. All were offering free sherry or tea parties to entice us into membership. So Sam and I decided to go to everything and to join nothing. We listened patiently to Marxists waxing eloquent about the struggle of the masses, Tories extolling the virtues of free enterprise, oarsmen talking tantalisingly about steaks for breakfast, and Scotsmen explaining how to breathe some Highland sanity in the midst of mad dogs and Englishmen. We even went to the Christian Union at four o'clock one day. No group was too ridiculous for us.

Like Sam, I was a cynical unbeliever – a humanist, as I called myself. My religious upbringing had been a little complicated. I had been brought up as a Christian Scientist, since my father had become one at the start of the First World War when it was fashionable among the intelligentsia. My father had been a classics scholar at Oxford, and the intriguing concept of the power of mind over matter had captured the imagination of many forceful personalities.

Almost the only thing I remember about Christian Science as a child was my Sunday School teacher telling a group of six-year-olds that if we had enough faith we could throw ourselves over a cliff and we would float down safely as if held by a parachute. This is not typical of Christian Science teaching, but it is all that I can remember to this day. Fortunately I never experimented, since I had no faith in my faith. My other memory was that my father never allowed a doctor near our home, since he believed there was no reality in any sickness: it was all a matter of the mind. When my father, a serving officer with the Royal Artillery, was away for many months at a time, my mother, a nominal Anglican, would surreptitiously ask a doctor to call when I had mumps or measles, but such medical interference would have been strongly disapproved of by my father.

So firm was he in his beliefs that when, in India, he was suffering from acute bronchial pneumonia, he refused all medical assistance – and died. The disease which supposedly had no reality killed him, and the human mind was an insufficient saviour.

I was ten at the time, and it was 1943, in the middle of the Second World War. My gentle, bereaved mother did the wisest thing she knew (for which I am now profoundly grateful) and had me quickly 'done' in the Anglican Church: I was baptized and confirmed, becoming a server in our parish church. Perhaps our local priest had never prepared a Christian Scientist for confirmation before, but I understood not a word of what he said, and found the sung eucharist every Sunday a ghastly dirge, which I assumed must be good for my soul since it was bad for everything else. For me it was all a meaningless religious mumbo-jumbo.

Inevitably, I suppose, I began to look for God, or at least for some kind of spiritual reality, in other directions. I took part in a few séances, curious to know if I could get in touch with my father. The experience left me not only disillusioned but with a cautionary awareness that I was dabbling in something dangerous. I now realise that every involvement with the occult (spiritualism, astrology, tarot cards, witchcraft and all the 'black arts') is like playing with an unexploded bomb. You never know when it may go off, and over the years I have had to counsel numerous people who, in one way or another, have been harmed – some of them seriously so – through occult experiences. It literally is a devilish business.

During my teenage years I tried a labyrinth of religious paths: theosophy, the teachings of Rudolf Steiner (since my uncle was a devotee of his), various forms of Buddhism, and was generally intrigued by the mysticism of Eastern religions. I once argued strenuously in a thesis for reincarnation since I found in this belief the only logical solution to the vexed question of suffering. But God was nowhere to be found – the Great Unreality in my life.

My school days were mostly enjoyable and I was satisfactorily successful, but all religious instruction was a total non-event from my point of view. Just once or twice I thought I glimpsed a fleeting shaft of spiritual light breaking through the dense fog of confusion. I was intrigued by a Franciscan monk giving a series of Lenten addresses. We all said, 'Wasn't his talk tremendous!' to give the impression that of course we understood every word; but like most of my friends, I am sure, I failed to grasp with any clarity anything at all. His brown 'dressing-gown' and open-toed sandals fascinated me, though I wondered how on earth anyone with any intelligence could go around like that for the sake of Christ. In fact, every contact with the Church reinforced my growing conviction, 'Not for me!'

The final straw came during my two years in the army. In other ways they were two marvellous years. Naturally there were a few less positive moments, such as when I sank my troop of self-propelled guns in a stinking German bog on the first day of massive military manoeuvres. I had surveyed the ground fairly quickly, so as to position four guns, giving covering fire for the infantry. The ground seemed somewhat squelchy, but in all other respects it was an excellent gun position. The guns swept it without too much difficulty; but when they 'tracked' to respond to different angles of fire, each gun crew reported in turn that they were beginning to sink. We simply had to pull out and find another position, which, had it been a real battle, would have been unpardonable. So we pulled out, only to discover that the ground on which they had been standing was the firmest in the whole area. As they moved forward they plunged into a thick black bog. The language I received from my superiors almost burnt out our entire radio communication system. I had never before or since seen tanks become submarines within a matter of seconds: it was immensely impressive, and I doubt if any other junior officer has accomplished the same feat with such dramatic effect.

But for most of my time in the army I made a lot of friends, played a great deal of sport, and went to countless parties including some eye-opening shockers in the red-light district of Hamburg, the Reeperbahn, notorious for its night clubs, brothels and strip shows. After one of the worst of these evenings, we were chased through the streets of Hamburg at about four in the morning. The German police cars had a tough time stopping our pepped-up Mercedes, though we eventually capitulated to about twelve of them. It was the nearest to a James Bond car chase that I have ever been in, and it was only our lack of sophisticated 007 equipment that caused us to lose. In one sense it was a breathtaking adventure; in reality it was a sordid, stupid, drunken dare which exposed the emptiness of our hearts. And every vacuum craves to be filled.

Army religion, however, certainly could not fill that inner void in my heart. Still on paper an Anglican, I went dutifully to the Regimental services – every decent officer was expected to do so – but the only active Christian I remember meeting throughout my entire two years was the Regimental Padre, who seemed by far the heaviest drinker in our regiment. Ten years later I discovered, through the then Chaplain General to the Forces, that our poor Padre had at that time been suffering a severe nervous breakdown. However, ignorant of that fact, I considered his behaviour my final proof of the futility of the Christian faith, and I became an atheist. Over the years I had found no spiritual reality, and it was a simple exercise to give myself philosophically satisfying arguments for saying 'There is no God!'

I can remember only one real prayer, if you can call it that, which I prayed during those years. After an especially wild party and while lying on my bed still dressed in my dinner jacket, and with a powerful hangover, I said aloud, 'O God, there must be a better life somewhere!'

Not by any stretch of the imagination did I remotely consider such a drunken heart-cry would be answered through that four o'clock tea-party organised by the Christian Union at Cambridge University. Sam would have said that I made two fatal mistakes that afternoon: I wore my old school tie, and I caught the speaker's eye on my way out.

After a nondescript tea-party, organised (I thought in my sophistication) by undergraduates with bright eyes, perpetual smiles and silly badges in their lapel buttonholes, we all had to sit down to listen to a young Anglican clergyman. I paid little attention to his words, since I did not believe in God anyway, though he stressed that the heart of the Christian faith was a personal relationship with Jesus Christ. I did not recall any-one ever saying that to me before, and I had reluctantly to admit that there was something unusually gracious and at-tractive about this clergyman. He spoke with simplicity and integrity, and unlike most other religious people I had so far met, seemed to speak from a genuine personal experience. It was not so much what he said, but who he was, that got through to me. In spite of all my prejudices and preconceived ideas, I could not help liking him. My cynicism was disturbed by the apparent reality of his faith. For that reason alone I gave him a polite smile as I made for the door, one of the first to leave.

Recognising my tie, he began to speak to me, and we soon discovered a number of mutual friends, some of whom had particularly impressed me by the quality of their lives, although I did not know for what reason. Gently but suddenly he turned the conversation.

'Forgive me for asking you a personal question. You may remember that a moment ago I talked about Christianity as a friendship with Jesus. Do you think that you know Jesus personally, or are you not quite sure about it?'

I was exceedingly embarrassed. In my own upper middle-class background, one never dreamt of asking such personal questions. Religion, if it existed at all, was purely a private affair. At the most one might discuss the Church, usually in highly arrogant and critical terms. But questions about one's personal faith were like questions about one's private sex life: it just wasn't done.

Neatly sidestepping his crash tackle I replied, 'I've been baptized and confirmed.' A good enough reply by any Anglican, I thought. But John Collins was not so easily diverted.

'If I had asked those mutual friends of ours that same question, they would have said Yes immediately,' he commented, again with that disturbingly disarming smile.

I thought back to those friends whom we had discussed a few moments before: Graeme, Michael, Peter. Although they had never once spoken to me about Christ at school, they had about them the same sort of attractiveness that I was beginning to find in John Collins. I realised that their professed faith in Christ could have been the common denominator. The trap was tightening.

Although I had won an exhibition in mathematics at Cambridge (physics and chemistry being my other major subjects), I was starting a degree course in Moral Sciences, which included philosophy, psychology, logic, ethics and metaphysics. Apart from my natural interest in those subjects, this was the humanist faculty in the university. But it also meant that I had some mental discipline in logical reasoning.

Logically it suddenly became as clear as a bell. I knew that this clergyman could not prove God. But equally, in spite of my professed atheism, I knew that I could not disprove God either. In logic, it might be true, it might not be true. If not true, forget it (as I had been doing for the last two or three years at least). But if it was true, I had to admit that it would be the most important truth in the universe. It simply could not be dismissed as irrelevant or unimportant.

'Would you like me to explain exactly how you can find God through Jesus Christ?' asked John Collins.

With my scientific training I knew that any honest seeker for truth ought at least to look at a hypothesis, especially if it seemed even remotely important. Further, if the hypothesis appeared reasonable, however unlikely, the right action would then be to experiment, to test the hypothesis for oneself. This is the very basis of all scientific research and the road to most forms of knowledge.

We agreed to have breakfast together the next day at the Garden House Hotel where he was staying. It was a sumptuous feast: fruit juice, kippers, eggs and bacon, toast, coffee – the lot, because John wanted as much time as possible to explain to me the way to God; and, although I did not realise it at the time, I was incredibly ignorant and confused about Christ and the Christian faith.

He began by asking if I felt any need of God. I could not honestly think of any need, apart from that impulsive cry when I was suffering from a hangover. But that surely was not enough. Perhaps in my more reflective moments I was not too sure of the purpose of my life. 'Is that what you mean by a need of God?' I asked John. He explained that a sense of purpose is certainly included, but that our primary need of God consists in our need for forgiveness. In countless ways we have broken God's laws, we have gone our own way, we have done our own thing. That is why God is naturally unreal in the experience of us all, until something is done about it. Surprisingly, I did not need much convincing about this. I knew there were some things in my life of which I was ashamed. I would not like the whole of my life to be exposed. I could also see that, logically, this was a possible explanation for the sense of God's remoteness and unreality. If he did exist and if I had turned my back on him, it followed that there would be a breakdown of communication.

'Yes,' I said after further discussion, 'I'm prepared to admit that I have sinned and so need forgiveness.'

John then described the next step as believing that Christ had died for my sins. 'Oh dear,' I thought to myself. 'Here are these religious clichés which don't mean a thing. Anyway, how can the death of Jesus all those years ago possibly have any relevance to me today?' John unexpectedly took a piece of toast and placed it on his upturned left hand.

'Let this hand represent you, and this toast represent your sin.' Looking at the semi-burnt piece of cold toast I thought it was a fair analogy. 'Now, let my right hand represent Jesus, who had no sin on him at all. There is a verse in the Bible which speaks about the cross like this: "All we like sheep have gone astray; we have turned every one to his own way; and the Lord (God in heaven) has laid on him (Jesus) the sin of us all".' (Isa. 53:6). As he said that, John transferred the toast from his left hand to his right hand. 'Now,' he said, once again with that winsome smile, almost like a chess player saying checkmate, 'where is your sin?'

My arrogant self despised the simplicity of it all; but logically it was as plain as could be.

'I suppose my sin is on Jesus,' I replied, going along with his analogy. In my heart I was beginning to see it, even though my mind wanted something much more intellectually profound. Perhaps that was the meaning of the cross. Perhaps Jesus did somehow take upon himself the sin and guilt of us all so that we, sinners though we all are, could be free to know the love and forgiveness of God, without any barrier at all. John referred to several other verses in the Bible which made exactly the same point.

'Next,' he said, 'you have to count the cost.' To put it simply I had to be willing to put right (with Christ's help) everything that I knew was wrong in my life, and be willing to put Christ first in my life. We discussed the implications of this for a time, and I could see that, if these things were true, there could be no half-measures. It must be all or nothing.

So we went to the final step to knowing God. John took me to a promise of Jesus that I had never heard before, from Revelation 3:20: 'Behold, I stand at the door and knock. If anyone hears my voice and opens the door I will come in.' We talked a little more, and I could see that faith simply means taking a person at their word. If, in prayer, I asked Jesus into my life, I had his promise that he would come in, and so make God real in my experience.

It all seemed far too simple, and there were still a host of philosophical questions as yet totally unanswered. But at least I understood the directions that John had given me.

'Let me suggest alternatives,' he said. 'Either we could go to my room and have a prayer together, or I could give you this booklet which sums up what I've been saying, and has a personal prayer at the end which you could make your own.'

I was much too embarrassed to pray with him then and there, and anyway I needed time to think. 'I'll take the booklet,' I said, and rose to make a hasty retreat, muttering something about being late for lectures.

'Just one more thing,' said John. 'If you do decide to pray that prayer, would you write to let me know that you've done it? I should be so grateful. Here's my address.'

Off I went, with my mind racing. I had gone to breakfast as a humanist, and now, just an hour or so later, I had the trembling excitement that I could be on the verge of a totally unexpected discovery. Or again, it could be yet another disillusionment which would only deepen my conviction as an atheist.

That evening, alone in my room, I read the booklet *Becoming a Christian* by John Stott, Rector of All Souls, Langham Place, London, where John Collins was a curate. The booklet was largely a summary of our breakfast conversation, but with all its simplicity it was compellingly clear in its logical reasoning. Steadily I realised that, if these things were true, I wanted them to become real in my own life. Awkwardly I slipped onto my knees beside my bed and prayed the prayer at the end of the booklet:

Lord Jesus Christ, *I humbly acknowledge* that I have sinned in my thinking and speaking and acting, that I am guilty of deliberate wrongdoing, and that my sins have separated me from Thy holy presence, and that I am helpless to commend myself to Thee;
I firmly believe that Thou didst die on the cross for my sins, bearing them in Thine own body and suffering in my place the condemnation they deserved;
I have thoughtfully counted the cost of following Thee. I

sincerely repent, turning from my past sins. I am willing to
surrender to Thee as my Lord and Master. Help me not to
be ashamed of Thee;
So now I come to Thee. I believe that for a long time Thou
hast been patiently standing outside the door knocking. I
now open the door. Come in, Lord Jesus, and be my
Saviour and my Lord for ever. Amen.

Absolutely nothing happened. No visions, no feelings, no
experiences, nothing. Everything seemed just the same as
before. I felt let down; and yet as I climbed into bed I had a
quiet sense of peace that I had done the right thing.

The next morning I again felt no different. And yet, what if
Christ really had come into my life? Would it matter if I
trusted his promise, at least for a day or two, to see if anything
happened? So I wrote a note to John Collins to say that I had
done it, and what next?

Two days later I had a charming reply to encourage me, and
he mentioned that he was asking a friend of his to call on me.
'Oh no!' I thought. 'I really have fallen into a religious trap' –
and I did not want to become religious. But I was astonished,
on my return from lectures that very same morning, to find a
hand-written note on my table.

For years I had been a cricket enthusiast; I was not a very
good performer (Captain of the Second XI at school was
about my standard), but of my various cricketing heroes,
none was greater than David Sheppard. With my studying at
Cambridge, living in Sussex and being English, the one
cricketer who evoked in me an enormous admiration was,
naturally, the person who had recently been Captain of
Cambridge, Sussex and England. On numerous occasions I
had seen him play: a magnificent opening batsman whose
command of the game was, for me, totally exhilarating. I
knew of nothing more exciting than watching David Sheppard
scoring runs with what seemed immense power and consum-
mate ease.

Imagine my astonishment, therefore, when I read this short
note on my table:

John Collins wrote this morning suggesting that I look you up. I will look in after lunch, but do not stay in especially.
   Yours, David Sheppard.

2

A Christian at Cambridge

'I don't think I have ever before met anyone who was so confused!' was David Sheppard's comment about me a few months later. Looking back I see now that my religious ideas were like a ball of wool after a playful kitten had been hard at work: an incredible tangle of various beliefs, interwoven with a few strands of Christianity here and there. Interestingly enough a very good friend of mine had given me, a few weeks before I went up to Cambridge, *The Imitation of Christ* by Thomas à Kempis, and this I had found both moving and stimulating, creating in me a measure of spiritual hunger. But my knowledge of the Gospel was effectively zero. I later discovered that I was not the only spiritually blind person. Jesus once said to a thoroughly religious and intelligent man, Nicodemus, 'Truly, truly I say to you, unless a man is born anew, he *cannot see* the kingdom of God' (John 3:3). The brilliant university scholar, Saul of Tarsus, said much the same thing: 'The unspiritual man does not receive the gifts of the Spirit of God, for they are folly to him, and he is not able to understand them because they are spiritually discerned' (1 Cor. 2:14). In more recent times, the eminent philosopher Bertrand Russell wrote a book called *Why I Am Not A Christian*, but it is clear from this book that he had little or no understanding of the basic truths of the Christian faith.

David Sheppard invited me round to his rooms at Ridley Hall, an Anglican theological college in Cambridge, where he was in his final year prior to ordination. Almost every week throughout the academic year I went round to talk to David, often for as much as three hours at a time, and he began to lay a foundation for my faith – or at least helped me to know the only foundation that will stand firm against every wind of doctrine and storm of life, the foundation of Jesus Christ. Normally we read a passage of the Bible together, David choosing a passage carefully each week to meet my particular need at that stage: Psalm 103 on assurance; Psalms 32 and 51 on repentance; Isaiah 53 on the cross; Luke 24 and I Corinthians 15 on the resurrection; James 1 on temptation; John 17 on prayer; Romans 12 on service; and so forth.

It is impossible to stress how vital these sessions were for me. Without them, humanly speaking, I should never have survived as a Christian. My first question, after asking Christ into my life, was, 'How on earth will I be able to keep this up? Won't it be like those useless New Year's resolutions all over again?' It had all faded after confirmation and after various other attempts to turn over a new religious leaf. What I had not realised was that, through the Spirit of God, I had started a new life. The first faint inklings of the reality of this were twofold: first, my army habit of swearing at about every fifth word ceased immediately; and second (much more important), a new love for people slowly began to dawn in my heart.

It was just as well! I had been an appalling snob, and must have been even more unpleasant in the eyes of other people than I am now! To begin with, I was proud of my family background. I had a long Scottish pedigree, my 'family tree' having been carefully researched back to the eleventh century. The Watsons lived for many centuries in Saughton, Edinburgh, and several of my ancestors are buried in Princes Street. One branch of the family, however, moved to the Lake District in 1537; and our family home was Calgarth Park, one mile north of Windermere, until it was handed over as a military hospital in the First World War. It was at one time a 3,000 acre estate, developed by Richard Watson, my great-great-great-grandfather. He married Dorothy le Fleming of Rydal Hall (now the Carlisle Diocesan Retreat Centre), so the family links with the Lake District were strong.

Richard Watson was an able and colourful character. He was born in 1737 and went to Trinity College, Cambridge in 1754. Within ten years, at the age of twenty-seven, he became Professor of Chemistry in the University although he admitted later in his own *Anecdotes*, 'At the time this honour was conferred on me I knew nothing at all of Chemistry and had never read a syllable on the subject, nor seen a single experiment in it.' After fourteen months of study in Paris, however, during which time he once destroyed his laboratory with an explosion, he returned to Cambridge to deliver 'a course of chemical lectures to a very full audience'. He wrote numerous scientific papers within the next two years and was promptly elected a Fellow of the Royal Society.

Only three years later, in 1771, the chair of Divinity became vacant, which Richard Watson considered 'the foremost post of learning in Europe'. He studied Divinity for one year, after which he was unanimously elected to the chair of Divinity although once again he admitted that he only 'knew as much of Divinity as could reasonably be expected of a man whose course of studies had been directed . . . to other pursuits'. Watson's writings as Regius Professor of Divinity were prolific, and probably his most important apologetic work was his *Apology for the Bible* published in 1796 in answer to 'the scurrilous abuse of the Scripture' contained in Thomas Paine's *Age of Reason. Apology for the Bible* was particularly well received, although when he handed it to King George III it is reputed that the King retorted, 'I never knew that the Bible needed an apology!' Nevertheless the King made Watson Bishop of Llandaff in 1782 – a bishopric that was the poorest in the country, but was considered by many of his contemporaries as a short stepping-stone for Watson to Canterbury. On a point of conscience, however, Watson clashed with both William Pitt and George III, who subsequently kept him at that safe distance in Wales, where he remained for thirty-four years. It was asked, 'If Watson, Bishop of Llandaff was factious and insolent, what might Watson, Archbishop of Canterbury or even Bishop of Durham, have become?'

It was from that background that I went to school at

Wellington College, where my father, uncles and cousins had all been educated, and then on to the 3rd Regiment of the Royal Horse Artillery, which was rightly proud of its traditions and outstanding military achievements. Understandably, perhaps, I had thoroughly imbibed what the Bible critically calls 'the pride of life', a human vanity based on privilege of birth or personal achievement, and which can prove a considerable stumbling-block to a true knowledge of God. The apostle Paul acknowledged that 'not many of noble birth' had been called by God, (1 Cor. 1:26). In fact God 'opposes the proud, but gives grace to the humble' (Jas. 4:6). These were painful and humbling lessons I had still to learn.

This new life that I had received, therefore, needed much nurturing. In his goodness, God gave me in David Sheppard someone I respected enormously, and it was mostly through his influence that I began to overcome some of my entrenched prejudices. Gently he encouraged me to get involved with the Christian Union in my college, St. John's. This I found extraordinarily difficult. Not only was the whole experience of Bible studies and prayer meetings totally foreign to me – I had not the slightest idea that such things existed and was initially shocked by their religious intensity – but on the surface I had nothing whatever in common with the other Christians in my college. Many of them came from very different backgrounds, and their interests were widely different as well. I read philosophy, and played hockey or squash seven days a week; most of them seemed to read chemistry, and played no sport at all. Today I find such differences quite irrelevant. What Christians have in common in Christ gloriously transcends all these worldly distinctions. But at the time I had almost to be pushed into fellowship with my Christian brothers, since I was afraid of becoming a religious fanatic by associating with them at all. I vividly remember one young man, when he prayed, gripping his chair in such agony that I genuinely thought he was suffering from serious constipation. 'What if my fellow officers from 3rd RHA could see me now!' I used to think to myself.

I was not the only one who was worried. I am not sure what

I wrote about all this to my mother, but she was clearly a little anxious that I had become religious, especially after my father's tragic death. Later I was requested to meet various family friends and relations to assure them that I wasn't rushing off to become a monk! My old school and army friends were frankly puzzled. They could not quite imagine the young officer who had drunk in night clubs in Hamburg now sitting in prayer meetings in Cambridge. 'It will soon pass,' they said charitably. 'Everyone goes through these phases at university. He'll probably be a Communist next term!'

Well, it didn't pass. Certainly I went through some agonies of doubt. A little time after my conversion I wrote in my diary, 'Is it all true, or am I making it up?' David Sheppard obviously saw that I was going through a difficult time, and we read that evening, as a devotional study, Psalm 103:

> Bless the Lord, O my soul;
>   and all that is within me, bless his holy name!
> Bless the Lord, O my soul,
>   and forget not all his benefits,
> who forgives all your iniquity,
>   who heals all your diseases,
> who redeems your life from the Pit,
>   who crowns you with steadfast love and mercy,
> who satisfies you with good as long as you live
>   so that your youth is renewed like the eagle's.

My intellectual questions remained unanswered, but the Spirit of God used this psalm to reassure me of God's love, and I was quietly conscious of his never-failing presence. The whole thing seemed so right and true. Here, surely, was something of the 'unsearchable riches of Christ' that countless millions of men and women had discovered all through the centuries. I worshipped God, my Father, through Jesus Christ, my Lord and Saviour.

I knew, of course, that a purely devotional faith would not be enough. If my philosophy lecturers mentioned God at all, they did so cynically, treating the whole subject as a curious historical debate that philosophers used to take seriously, but not, of course, in this age of logical positivism and linguistic analysis. The issues of today had long by-passed any medieval fantasies about God. I was fortunate, however, in having as my psychology supervisor Malcolm Jeeves (at present Professor of Psychology at St. Andrews University), who was and is a deeply committed Christian and who helped me to integrate my faith and intellect. I began to see, for example, the basic difference between the meaning and the mechanism of something. Even if a 'conversion experience' could be described in psychological terms, this in no way invalidated the meaning or significance of it. The significance of an item of news on the television is not at all affected by a detailed scientific description of how a television set works.

I also came to see that there are different forms of knowledge, all of which depend, at least in part, on faith. There is logical or mathematical knowledge; and providing I accept by faith the fundamental principles of mathematics, I gain further knowledge by sheer logical reasoning. Then there is scientific or experimental knowledge; and providing I accept by faith the laws of science, I gain further knowledge by testing hypotheses with empirical investigation. There is also personal knowledge, or the knowledge of persons, which is quite different from either mathematical or scientific knowledge. You can never 'prove' a person. You can only know a person; and you can know a person only if you commit yourself to that person. I realised that the same was true of God. I saw that no scientific world-view, however complete it might one day become, could affect our knowledge of God one way or another. These were some of the issues I was trying to come to terms with in the process of deepening my own relationship with Christ.

An important milestone came when I helped my best friend to find Christ for himself. Tom was a delightful person, amusing, generous, a gifted sportsman, and in every way charming. David Sheppard had carefully taught me within a week or two of my own conversion how to lead someone to

Christ, and so I shared what I could with Tom, who was obviously interested. I am sure that I put it rather badly, but through the help of a visiting preacher to Cambridge, Maurice Wood (now Bishop of Norwich), Tom accepted Christ into his life. I was so overjoyed I literally could not sleep a wink all night, and I have never lost the sense of deep joy and immense privilege in helping someone find God. Tom joined me in my weekly sessions with David Sheppard, and I found all this a huge encouragement to my own struggling faith.

I could see, however, that Tom was still weighing up the cost of true Christian discipleship very cautiously. For him, the account in the Gospels of the meeting between the rich young ruler and Jesus was all-important. Tom was disturbed by the clear instruction Jesus gave to that man to sell everything he had before he could follow him. I told Tom that I was sure that this instruction did not apply to everyone (I felt much too threatened to imagine that it did, anyway), but that riches were the special idol in that young ruler's life, and therefore he needed an unusual and particular challenge before Jesus could be his Lord as well as his Saviour. Tom, however, took the command of Christ both literally and seriously. In order to follow Christ with integrity, he thought, he would have to give up everything. Perhaps in Tom's life there were particular issues that he had to face – there are in most of our lives. But over the first Christmas vacation Tom found the continuous round of social engagements too appealing, and he seemed to surrender his faith.

I have no doubt that Tom was being thoroughly honest with himself. He rightly hated hypocrisy. However, after his conversion we had agreed to share rooms together, only to find that we were now disagreed on what was fast becoming the most important element in my life. Although we still remained very good friends, I personally found this an extremely testing time, although it increased my resolve to put Christ first, whether others came with me or not.

Partly for these reasons I developed a fairly disciplined faith from the start. Having overcome some of my initial culture shock at the 'fanaticism' of those who took the

Christian faith seriously, I began to order my life according to rules that I set myself. Every morning, without fail, I would read my Bible and pray for forty-five minutes at least. I had a rapidly growing list of people and needs that I felt I ought to pray for. Every week I learnt six verses from the Bible, together with their references, and revised the ones I had previously learnt. I began to devour Christian books, reading concurrently a doctrinal, a biographical and a devotional book, in order to feed on a balanced diet. I was committed in terms of Christian fellowship (though I found prayer meetings difficult for a long time), and active in evangelism, taking many friends to evangelistic services and seeing some of them come to Christ. On the negative side I was equally strong. Having experienced the bitterness of some of the forbidden fruits in the world, I decided not to smoke (not that I did anyway), not to drink, not to dance and not to go to cinemas or theatres. Having tasted the new wine of the Spirit, the old wine of the flesh seemed like luke-warm water, and I spat it out of my mouth. Some of my new way of life was certainly too legalistic, but to this day I am grateful for that early note of discipline in an age when such words are no longer fashionable. It provided a rock-like foundation, on which the superstructure could later afford to be more flexible.

Not that everything was quite so pious and simple as it may have seemed. For all my new-found fervour, the one event that I dreaded was an open-air service at the end of the summer term organised by the Christian Union, at The Mill. The Mill was a popular pub by the river where most of my pagan friends spent their Sunday lunch-times drinking beer. On a sunny day there was always a crowd there, hence it was a good target for the Christian Union's open-air service. But however real my ardour for Christ had become, it unquestionably did not stretch to soap-box oratory to my beer-drinking friends.

'Will you be there with us?' pressed my Christian brethren.

'I'm not sure yet,' had been my evasive reply. Imagine my relief when another friend invited me to lunch in his rooms for that very same Sunday. His sister would be there, and I had a

sneaking suspicion that this friend hoped I might fall in love
with her. She was a delightful girl anyway, so I readily
accepted the invitation. What a perfect excuse for missing the
service! However, when I arrived at my friend's rooms he
said, 'It's such a glorious day, let's get a punt at The Mill and
go for a picnic.'

The inevitable happened. I arrived at The Mill, which was
now thronged with students, including many from the Christian Union who were immediately conspicuous in their Sunday
best. When some of them saw me they were thrilled. They
were clearly not so thrilled when I climbed into a punt with my
friend and his sister, and pushed off for a picnic. Even worse,
when we were some way down the river towards Granchester,
my friend (always a tactician) made some excuse about having
to do some work, and jumped off the punt to run back to his
college. That left me alone with his sister, wondering how on
earth I was to get back to the pub without entirely losing face
with my Christian friends. There was no way out of it; so back
we came, like any other romantic couple on the river that day,
arriving at The Mill when the evangelistic thrust of the
Christian Union was at its climax. I suspect that I became the
object of some fervent prayer for the next few weeks, and my
promising friendship with this charming girl came abruptly to
an end. I fear that, in my embarrassment, I was ungracious
and rude. Many readjustments to my new life in Christ had
yet to be made.

Churchgoing had always been a terrible chore for me:
something of a penance which I had assumed Christians
thought necessary to atone for all their many sins. Escorted by
David Sheppard, I began to go to various services where the
form was usually familiar, but the Spirit altogether different. I
had never before seen so many young people singing hymns
and praying prayers as though they really meant them! And
the sermons, although some were in biblical jargon which I
found incomprehensible, were mostly informative, personal
and helpful. I was however horrified by the first evangelistic
sermon I heard, only a few days after my conversion: there
was far too much hell-fire and judgment for my liking, and I

was astonished by queues of undergraduates going up to the preacher afterwards to say that they had accepted Christ. I was so glad I had done it quietly on my own earlier in the week. Never in a thousand years, I thought, would I have joined such a queue of converts. Later I found the constant proclamation of the Gospel, by visiting preachers every Sunday evening in Holy Trinity Church, utterly enthralling, and totally failed to see why some of the many friends I took with me could not embrace Christ there and then. Altogether, it was an exhilarating time of rapid growth.

My first Christmas vacation proved another important milestone, for two main reasons. First, I had the tremendous joy of leading my mother to Christ. We had never talked together about personal matters with ease; but her second marriage, after my father's death, had been difficult, and she was aware of the need of God's help for several reasons. Very simply I outlined the steps I had taken to find Christ, and prayed with her, phrase by phrase, as I helped her to ask Christ into her life. It was wonderful to see her begin to read her Bible and to pray, and I could soon see the difference that Christ was making in her life.

Then, after Christmas, David Sheppard had persuaded me to go as a helper to a boys' camp (or houseparty as it really was), run by the Rev. E. J. H. Nash, affectionately known as Bash. David had to apply some pressure on me, as I had planned to go on a skiing holiday with Tom, two other male friends of ours and four stunningly beautiful girls, one being Britain's top model at that time. I suspect that David saw this as a real and obvious temptation for me, the flesh fighting hard against the Spirit. The Spirit won – but not without a struggle.

After my leadership experience at school and in the army I felt sure that I was just the kind of leader these boys' camps were needing, so I looked forward to organising some activities for them. In fact, I spent almost the entire time peeling potatoes, sweeping floors and scrubbing pots and pans. Imagine doing that instead of skiing with four beautiful girls! I must be crazy! However, that camp, and the next one at

3

Theology

With David Sheppard as my spiritual mentor, it was perhaps a little too obvious that I should think in terms of ordination. I had arrived at Cambridge with no clear plans about my future. I had vaguely thought of the Foreign Office, but it had all been a distant dream. What about the ordained ministry in the Anglican Church? David asked me if I had considered it.

There were a few immediate objections. Some relatives and friends of my family were not enthusiastic. For them, ordination was only for those who could not think of anything better to do. 'I suppose if you became a bishop it might just be all right,' commented one. Better wisdom came from some older Christians who were beginning to know me. Fearing that I might simply be copying the example of David Sheppard, they strongly suggested a teaching profession instead: 'There is a lot of excellent work you can do as a Christian master in a school,' they said; and indeed I had thoroughly enjoyed a term teaching at Wellington College just before going to Cambridge.

The primary obstacle to ordination, however, was a personal one. I was terrified at the thought of having to speak in public. Shouting orders to a troop of soldiers on parade was one thing; the thought of having to preach a sermon almost paralysed me with fear. The first talk on the Christian faith I ever gave lasted for a nightmarish five minutes. My mouth was dry, my knees knocking, my hands shaking. I thought I would never make it.

'The trouble is,' I protested to David Sheppard, 'I wouldn't know what to preach about.'

'More likely,' David countered, 'when you really begin to know your Bible, you won't know what *not* to preach about!' I was far from convinced.

It was not until Trinity Sunday 1955 that I first attended a service in King's College Chapel. I am not sure why I went, except that most undergraduates go at some time or other because of the beauty of the building and the excellence of the choir. But apart from enjoying the aesthetic magic of the whole occasion, I was completely riveted by an unemotional but powerful sermon on the need of men for the ordained ministry. I had no idea who the preacher was, but later discovered that he had been the Rev. Cyril Bowles, then the Principal of Ridley Hall and now Bishop of Derby. Through him God spoke so directly to me that the call to the ministry, which had been growing slowly stronger over the months, was now abundantly clear. I applied to the selection board of the Church of England, and was duly accepted as a candidate for ordination.

After two years studying philosophy, psychology, logics, ethics and metaphysics, when I did reasonably well in the exams in spite of my increasing preoccupation with Christian work (and still a lot of sport), I changed to theology. As still a very young Christian I found most of the lectures difficult and disturbing. I discovered that it was theology, and not philosophy as Keats had suggested, that could 'clip an angel's wings, unweave a rainbow'. Much of the dry, dusty stuff that we were studying seemed thoroughly destructive. What on earth did it have to do with the knowledge of God? Not that the theological scene was entirely bleak. There was always the saintliness of Professor Charlie Moule that shone radiantly through his lectures, and significantly he began each series with humble prayer, submitting himself to the authority of God and his word. I admired Professor Owen Chadwick for his immense scholarship, combined with a gentle and dry sense of humour. And Professor Henry Chadwick made the theological controversies of the early Church live in an astonishing way, impersonating the fathers and heretics as though he had known each one of them.

However, apart from these, few lecturers spoke with any conviction. One man, who was insufferably boring, used to begin most of his sentences like this: 'It is not unreasonable to suppose that it might not be the case that these two events were not unconnected.' I used to sit there counting the negatives in each sentence on my fingers, to find out whether the final statement was positive or negative. Matthew's comment about Jesus, at the end of the Sermon on the Mount, came home with fresh force: 'When Jesus had finished his discourse the people were astonished at his teaching; unlike their own teachers he taught with a note of authority.'

In sweeping contrast to the dithering caution of most academic theologians, who were efficiently undermining the faith of some of my friends, Billy Graham led a mission to the university in November 1955. Interestingly, when he tried, somewhat unsuccessfully, to be academic, his preaching lacked power. But when he accepted the apparent foolishness of the message of 'Christ crucified' and preached it with simplicity and integrity, the power of God's Spirit was manifestly at work, changing the lives of many undergraduates. It was a lesson I have never forgotten. I had first to work through the vital question of the authority of the Scriptures as the word of God; since then it has been my constant desire over the years to build faith. I could well understand the complaint of Goethe, a self-confessed agnostic, who once said to a preacher: 'You tell me of your certainties; I've enough doubts of my own.'

Any preacher or theologian may of course go through times of agonising doubt, even over the most basic issues of the Gospel; if so, he should share these with a few friends, not preach them from a pulpit or publish them in paperback. I was a curate in Cambridge when John Robinson's book *Honest to God* came out. It seems that it was written during a 'dark night of the soul' in John Robinson's life, and most Christians experience such deep questionings. Perhaps there were no friends close enough to him to help at the time. But such doubts published in popular book form did untold damage. When the psalmist was totally baffled by God's seeming inactivity in the face of suffering, he wisely kept silent: 'If I had said, "I will speak thus," I would have been untrue to the generation of thy children.' (Ps. 73:15). Declaring his doubts publicly would not have helped anyone.

G. K. Chesterton's words are still very much to the point, in an age when it is fashionable for some preachers to express their humility by saying how much they do not know: 'What we suffer from today is humility in the wrong place. Modesty has settled upon the organ of conviction, where it was never meant to be. A man was meant to be doubtful about himself, but undoubting about the truth; this has been exactly reversed.'

It would be wrong to conclude that I thought my theological studies a waste of time. Apart from the enormous gain I received from Professors Moule, Chadwick and Chadwick, it was invaluable being made to think through carefully most of the basic issues of the Christian faith. How far could the Bible be trusted as the word of God? What was the nature of its inspiration and authority? Why was the cross so central to the faith? What was the atoning work of Christ? How convincing was the evidence for the resurrection? Indeed, how sure could we be about anything, concerning matters of faith?

When preparing for an essay I would be given a long list of books to read, and I knew that some of them might be hefty intellectual attacks on, say, the authority of Scripture. I then asked one or two academic theologians whose personal beliefs were similar to my own for another list of books on the same subject written by scholars taking a much more conservative and orthodox view. I would then read at least a few books from 'both sides' and try to balance my essays with arguments and counter-arguments. It was hard work, but in this way I tried to tackle the critical questions seriously without being 'tossed to and fro by every wind of doctrine' or theological fashion. Through this process I became intellectually even more convinced of the great themes of the Christian Gospel, and this was important for a healthy growth in

Christ. We are to love God with all our *mind* as well as with all our heart and soul and strength. During this time I also remembered a shrewd principle that someone once gave me: 'Never let what you don't know shake your confidence in what you do know.' I certainly did not have all the answers to various intellectual questions, and yet all the time I was clearly growing in my knowledge of Christ.

Undoubtedly the most formative influence on my faith during the five years at Cambridge was my involvement with the boys' houseparties, or 'Bash camps' as they were generally known. Over the five years I went to no less than thirty-five of these camps: two at Christmas, two at Easter and three in the summer of each year. They were tremendous opportunities for learning the very basics of Christian ministry. Through patient and detailed discipling (although that word was never used) I learned, until it became second nature, how to lead a person to Christ, how to answer common questions, how to follow up a young convert, how to lead a group Bible study, how to give a Bible study to others, how to prepare and give a talk, how to pray, how to teach others to pray, how to write encouraging letters, how to know God's guidance, how to overcome temptation, and also, most important, how to laugh and have fun as a Christian – how not to become too intense, if you like. I also gained excellent grounding in basic Christian doctrines, with strong emphasis being placed on clarity and simplicity. All this was being constantly modelled by those who were much more mature in the faith, and I may never fully realise how much I owe to the amazing, detailed, personal help that I received over those five years. No Christian organisation is perfect, of course; and it would be easy to find fault with a group as powerful and as effective as this one. But if God has given me a useful ministry in any area today, the roots of it were almost certainly planted during those remarkable five years in the camps. It was the best possible training I could have received.

Sadly, I was not so receptive during my two years at theological college, Ridley Hall, which largely through my own fault was such a difficult and negative time. With the combined influence of the Christian Union at Cambridge and these boys' camps, I had developed strong evangelical convictions, and was thus deeply suspicious about everything else within the Christian Church. In my spiritual immaturity, my faculties had not yet been 'trained by practice to distinguish good from evil' (Heb. 5:14). I disliked the formality of Ridley chapel services every day; I rejected any teaching that I considered remotely 'liberal'; I found the staff giving theoretical answers to questions I was not yet asking; and my foremost priority was still my evangelistic work in the university, often at the expense of activities at Ridley Hall, most of which I regarded as interfering with the real work I felt called to do. The staff were patient with my spiritual arrogance and critical attitudes, and I am sure now that I would have grown in my knowledge of God far more had I been a little more humble and positive in my approach. I have since met many students at theological colleges and seminaries of all traditions who are as critical and defensive as I was, digging in behind their own convictions for safety and not being open to other ways in which God may be at work within his world-wide church. Much of this is the inevitable mark of immaturity.

At the same time, serious questions are today being asked (and rightly so) about the most helpful methods of training men and women for the ministry of the Church. More emphasis is being placed (and in my opinion still needs to be placed) on first-hand experience of church work as part of the training. This was the method of Jesus who lived and worked with his disciples. They watched him on the job, listened to him, were sent out by him, reported back to him, learnt from their mistakes, and so on. It was not 'first theory, then practice'. The learning and doing were closely interwoven. They were called primarily to be 'with him', and in this way he prepared them for the most effective leadership that the Church has ever known. There are surely lessons here for every theological college and seminary.

My real training for ministry, therefore, developed during my first curacy in a thoroughly different environment. John

Collins, then Vicar of St. Mark's Church, Gillingham in Kent, invited me to be his curate. So, from the cultured atmosphere of Cambridge I moved, almost five years to the day after my conversion, to the tough dockyard parish in Gillingham. What would be the effect of the Gospel I had discovered in Cambridge in a different culture altogether?

4

St. Mark's, Gillingham

'You'll especially enjoy the Youth Club,' John Collins told me, encouragingly. 'David MacInnes has done amazing work there.'

David MacInnes, whom I had come to know at Cambridge and liked very much, was the other bachelor curate who joined John and Diana Collins when they started at Gillingham two years before. For financial reasons we all lived in the Victorian vicarage, together with the Collins's two young children, a Swiss *au pair* girl and Graham Scott-Brown, a brilliant young doctor who was preparing to go to Nepal as a missionary. It was quite a party! We had a marvellous time praying, planning, studying and working together. Many things were beginning to happen in the parish, and so almost every day there were developments to encourage us, or battles to be fought.

It was a privilege to enjoy such close fellowship. We avoided the snare common to many Christians working in tough situations, namely loneliness, and we certainly had lots of fun together. For instance, with various meetings almost every evening until quite late, John, David, Graham (for a few months) and I used to cook a light supper after Diana had wisely retired to bed. I became an expert at omelettes (and nothing else), and calculated that I must have cooked at least 1,000 omelettes during my three years there. For one week we tried to vary the menu with cauliflower cheese made in a pressure cooker; but Diana protested that the smell wafting upstairs was like the Russian army taking its boots off, so back we went to omelettes!

I quickly discovered that the bed-sitting rooms which David and I occupied, just inside the front door, were also the main meeting rooms for the parish: Confirmation Candidates, Young Wives, Pathfinders, Sunday School, Mothers' Union, Youth Fellowship, Christian Night School, and so on; and because of the complexity of various meetings and the short-age of stackable chairs, my first six months in the parish seemed largely taken up with moving forty chairs, several times a week, from the hall five hundred yards down the road to our respective rooms, and then back to the hall again. I felt just like a furniture remover! Was I really ordained for this, I wondered? It was much like scrubbing those pots and pans at the boys' camps; and ever since then I have looked for willingness to serve in simple, menial tasks, as an important qualification for spiritual leadership.

David MacInnes had indeed done magnificent work in the Youth Club, although I felt that John was exaggerating considerably when he said that I would enjoy it. At times I was simply terrified, although I tried hard not to show it. Always it was challenging, and afterwards we could have a good laugh; but David had attracted some lively gangs of teddy-boys (as they were then called), who thought nothing of having a good punch-up or carving one another up with razors, broken glass, flick-knives, or any other weapons available. This was not what I was used to at St. John's College, Cambridge. David had a terrific sense of humour which these tough lads – and lasses – obviously enjoyed, and was thus able to exercise effective control without antagonis-ing potential trouble-makers to the point of violence. He won the respect of virtually everyone who came to that club (we usually had about 140 there each Friday evening) and his fifteen-minute talks during the club epilogues at the end of each evening were quite brilliant. David and I became very close friends, and have continued such ever since, so I was only too glad when he was there running the club, with me playing a minor role, and I always felt distinctly inferior

whenever he was away. Every Friday, before going down to
the club, I would go on my knees and pray over the relevant
verses from Jeremiah 1: 'Be not afraid of their faces, for I am
with you to deliver you, says the Lord.'

During my three years at Gillingham we never actually had
a fight in the club, but several times came very near to one.
One night, when David was speaking elsewhere, I noticed
two rival gangs present, each with about twelve members. I
kept a close watch on them; but when I was in another room
talking to someone else, the two gangs slipped out of the club.
'There's a fight brewing outside!' I was told. So I rushed out of
the door only to find, in the small courtyard at the bottom of
the steps, the two gangs lined up on either side ready to charge
at each other and equipped with a variety of ugly weapons.
Without thinking I raced down the steps into the middle of
them, and with an authority which surprised even me I told
them that on no account could they fight on these premises,
since this was a Christian club. I was obviously in a highly
vulnerable position, but they accepted my word, and after a
few tense minutes walked away. Later I heard, with much
sadness, that they had gone to a nearby common and there
fought a pitched battle, several of them ending up in hospital.

I am not sure that I ever 'enjoyed' the Youth Club,
although we had some hilarious moments, often at the expense of visiting speakers. Through David's undoubted skill I
gradually learned a few tricks of the trade, but any speaker
had to keep his wits about him. We had a few battered sofas
and armchairs which were pulled up for the front row of an
audience for the epilogue, and some of the lads would pull out
long chunks of stuffing from these chairs, and push them into
their ears as soon as the speaker started his talk. Also, if we
failed to get all cigarettes extinguished in time for the talk,
someone would blow huge smoke-rings across the speaker's
face. These rings were always fascinating to watch as they
floated in front of us all, and guaranteed to upset all but the
most gifted speaker. Others would stuff their pockets with
snooker balls immediately prior to the epilogue, and roll them
noisily across the bumpy wooden floor. Occasionally a small

coin or piece of silver paper would be pushed in at the bottom
of a light bulb, so that when the lights were turned on
everything fused.

Every summer we would take between seventy and eighty
young people for a week's houseparty; and although the
majority of those who came had already been won for Christ
through the club, life could still be difficult. God never
eliminates our personalities, and our Christian members were
just as lively as the others. Unfortunately for David and
myself endless practical jokes were played – many of them
neither practical nor funny, at least not for us! Our cars
regularly disappeared, or the wheels were removed from
them. I had everything put into my bed from black coal and
damp sand to live frogs. And yet these weeks were always
magnificent times. Whatever else could be said about the
Youth Club, it was never, never dull. Most of the families in
Gillingham had moved originally from the East End of London, and so there was a sharp cockney wit which kept us on
our toes all the time. I also developed an enormous affection
for numerous individuals and families, and it was wonderful seeing the power of Christ changing the lives of so
many.

Of course there were casualties, in more ways than one.
When one dockyard apprentice found Christ, he was beaten
up by his mates in the dockyard the next day, and was in
hospital for four days. Thankfully he stood his ground well,
and is today a fine Christian leader. Others had too close an
identity with the group from which they were converted; and
although we spent many hours with them, the pressure of the
group proved too much for some, and they fell away from
Christ. We also made the mistake of allowing quite young
Christians to give their testimonies of conversion too often.
They had committed almost every crime in the book before
their conversion, and therefore their stories were both dramatic and popular. But those who gave their testimonies
invariably went through spiritual attacks later, and some
tragically gave up their faith. There were many disappointments, but Christ became real for a growing number, and we

often took small teams to other clubs for effective evangelistic evenings. On the whole we were the toughest and liveliest club in the area, so our visits were always popular, and David and I found that the time we spent with these young people, doing all sorts of things together, was always profitable.

In countless other ways I had much to learn. Giving short talks at a camp for public schoolboys was quite different from preaching in a large Victorian church in a dockyard area. Here, both John and Diana Collins were superb 'tutors'. Diana, having been trained as an actress at the Royal Academy of Dramatic Art, worked hard on my voice, trying to change it from the sound of an army officer on parade to something more fitting for a pulpit. She had me first relaxing on the floor and then making all sorts of extraordinary noises which reverberated round the vicarage, much to the amusement (or annoyance) of others who lived there. I found her exercises an enormous help, and it is sad that so few preachers have any guidance concerning the use of the one 'instrument' they are playing all the time.

John too gave me invaluable training, and his curates have always been known as some of the best-trained clergy in the Church of England. After every sermon I preached, John would take the time and trouble to comment thoughtfully on both the points that were good and those that were not so good. He never made more than about three critical comments on any one sermon (even if he could think of thirty-three), so that I was never discouraged. Indeed he was a great encourager all the time; and with his and David's preaching setting me an extremely high standard, I found these years the best training that I could have found in any parish. Over and over again I was astonished to hear from my friends who were curates in other parishes that very few received any practical training at all, and all too often very little encouragement. The work of training others is perhaps the most important work that any Christian leader can do. Both John and Diana have always been marvellous enablers, spotting the potential in others and working hard to develop that potential to its full. It is doubtless for that reason, among others, that the churches they have served have always been unusually blessed by God.

Life in Gillingham was frequently rewarding and we had lots of fun together; but it was never easy. At times it could even be dangerous. One particular night we were attacked in the vicarage by a wild and drunken Irishman. He was well known in the area, as it was alleged that he had shot at his wife with a double-barrelled shot-gun, but fortunately missed. We had given shelter to his wife and children in the past and the man had often been belligerent. On this occasion he was for some reason convinced that we were sheltering his wife again. Although we assured him that we were not, he broke two windows in the vicarage, smashed down a door or two, and by the time the police arrived (we had dialled 999 several times!), the man had in his hands a huge boulder. Inside the vicarage we were pretty scared and had armed ourselves as best we could. I had a broom, John a baseball bat, and Paul Russell (David MacInnes's successor) the ebony statue of an African girl. Diana, the most resourceful of us all, was in the bathroom upstairs pouring jugs of cold water from the window onto the man's head as he tried to smash his way through the front door. In court later on the man said, 'Your Honour, I remember it was raining at the time!'

Among other outstanding memories of that first curacy, a week's visit from that remarkable and courageous Dutch-woman, Corrie ten Boom, was a definite highlight. Knowing that she would be staying with us in the vicarage, we were all a little nervous because of the reputation of her amazing min-istry, not only in Ravensbrück Concentration Camp, but throughout Germany after the war. God had particularly used her to release people from satanic powers, and the Nazi reign of terror had been literally a devilish inspiration, partly through heavy involvement with the occult. Hitler often spoke of being guided by voices within him, and was surely devil-inspired, if not devil-possessed. So with Corrie's record of helping those who had been troubled by evil spirits, we just wondered what she might find in an English vicarage! As it transpired, Corrie was the most wonderful, gracious and normal guest you could possibly have imagined. It was hard to think of her suffering all the brutalities of a Nazi concentration camp. She seemed so gentle, so good, and with a delightful sense of humour. Her talks, illustrated by simple and unforgettable visual aids, made a lasting impression on us all. Most of all, she was someone who walked daily with her Heavenly Father; and sometimes in conversation, while we were expressing some anxiety about something, she would turn so naturally to prayer that it took us a few moments to realise that she was talking no longer to us, but to God.

When John, David and I were seeing her off by train, from a crowded Gillingham platform, Corrie wanted to say something to us that we would remember. As the train moved slowly out of the station, she put her head through the carriage window and shouted at us, 'Don't wrestle, just nestle!' All eyes turned towards us, three clergymen, formally dressed in our clerical collars with our faces turning a delicate shade of pink. But I have never forgotten that simple slogan, even if, in practice, I have not always found it easy to rest quietly in the love and peace of the Lord. But God wants all of us to develop a simple trust in the Father's loving care, a trust that Corrie learnt through appalling suffering and grief.

After three years at St. Mark's, Gillingham, I went back to Cambridge for my second curacy, deliberately accepting an invitation to a totally different parish, the Round Church, for the purpose of widening my experience. I had no idea that the next three years would contain some of the most thrilling, confusing, traumatic and painful experiences of my life.

5

Spiritual Renewal

From the very start in Cambridge I became unexpectedly depressed. It was not a severe depression; but even though I had exchanged the relative ugliness of a dockyard town for the outstanding beauty of Cambridge, as I lived and worked in the heart of the finest university in the world (I may be a little prejudiced), I missed the vitality of Gillingham more than I had imagined possible.

Mark Ruston, my vicar, whom I had known well from my previous five years in Cambridge, could not have been more thoughtful and caring, and his steady and faithful ministry for Christ has been one of the outstanding features in Cambridge for over twenty-seven years. However, in sharp contrast to the lively wit of Gillingham, Cambridge as a town seemed remarkably dull. Even the church services, compared with Gillingham, seemed dull. They had little spark about them. Parish prayer meetings felt the same: heavy and depressing. I have never been very patient, and I was aching for some spark of life, just a little enthusiasm, something, whatever it might be, to make God seem more real in our midst. There was nothing wrong with the teaching: it was simple and biblical, and obviously helpful to scores of people. But oh, for some fire of the Spirit!

Looking back, I believe that God used my youthful impatience to spur me into a series of personal studies that proved a major turning-point in my life and ministry. I started to read the great histories of revival, fascinated by the outpouring of God's Spirit on groups of men and women at different times

and in different places. Many of the manifestations of revival
were totally strange to me, with people weeping before God,
prostrate before him, crying out for mercy, sometimes for
hours on end. It was hard to discern the sovereign work of the
Spirit of God from human hysteria or infectious enthusiasm.
But clearly something remarkable had happened in the times
of Jonathan Edwards, Wesley and Whitefield, in the eighteenth century, the Revival of 1800, the Awakening of 1858,
the Welsh Revival of 1904, and the Hebrides Revival of
1949, not to mention numerous others. I wished that
God could send us another revival, not least here in Cambridge; and I began to pray seriously about this, sometimes
joining forces with the Rev. Herbert Carson, Vicar of
St. Paul's, and Dr. Basil Atkinson, Senior Librarian at the
University.

Next, I studied again the Acts of the Apostles, and the
conviction was steadily dawning on me that there was a
normal spiritual dynamic about the early Church that was
almost entirely missing within the Church of today. Even in
Gillingham we seemed to have been on a different spiritual
wavelength altogether. I remember there studying in our staff
meetings 1 Corinthians 12 and 14, where the apostle Paul
writes fully about the gifts of the Holy Spirit, especially
prophecy and tongues, and we simply had no idea at all what
he was talking about.

We took the usual evangelical line that all such gifts were
purely for the apostolic period and were not even meant for
today. But then why were such specific instructions given for
their use within the pages of the New Testament? And what
about those strange Pentecostals, whose growth in South
America, in particular, had been one of the most remarkable
Christian movements of this century? Had they experienced
the power and gifts of the Spirit that we were somehow
missing? These became insistent, urgent questions that I
could not escape.

At the same time I was doing a detailed Bible study on the
nature of faith. I could see, in example after example, that
God's unusual demonstrations of power came when men and

women dared to take him at his word, whether they under-stood it all or not. For example, in the Christmas story, the Virgin Mary is promised a gift of a son who will be 'the Son of the Most High . . .' She is puzzled: 'How can this be, since I have no husband?' Once again the promise is given: 'The Holy Spirit will come upon you, and the power of the Most High will overshadow you . . .' So she accepts the promise of God at its face value, and responds in two very important ways. First, she surrenders her life completely to God: 'Be-hold, I am the handmaid of the Lord; let it be to me according to your word.' And then, amazingly, she begins to praise God that it is *already true*, even though the reality of the actual experience is still to come. In the *Magnificat* or the *Song of Mary*, she bursts out in praise:

> My soul magnifies the Lord,
> and my spirit rejoices in God my Saviour,
> for he has regarded the low estate of his handmaiden.
> For behold, henceforth all generations will call me blessed;
> for he who is mighty *has done* great things for me . . .

As far as Mary is concerned, it is already true as soon as the promise has been given.

Now that is faith, and I began to realise how often we limit God to our own narrow human understanding, or else to a specifically scientific world-view. Why should we not take him more seriously at his word, whether we understand it or not, whether we immediately experience it or not?

Most significant of all, I began a series of meditations in the Beatitudes, from the Sermon on the Mount. I had been inspired to do this after reading two volumes of expository sermons on Matthew 5–7 by Dr. Martyn Lloyd-Jones. I found that over a period of three or four months God was taking me through the first four Beatitudes in terms of my spiritual experience. It was a painful and humbling business.

Blessed are the poor in spirit. The word for 'poor' in the Greek is a strong word, meaning poverty-stricken or bank-rupt. It comes from a word meaning 'to cringe'. In other words, a man is so overwhelmed by a sense of poverty that he is beaten to his knees and has to throw himself on the mercy of God. To begin with, this was a far cry from my own opinions about myself. After a fairly 'successful' first curacy, I was coming to the conclusion that I had more or less 'arrived'. I was well taught in Christian doctrine and practice, and thought it was my task for the rest of my life to go on preaching the truth and to correct those who disagreed with me! I had also made some sweeping judgments about the dullness and heaviness of the services at the Round Church. So God began to rebuke me for my spiritual pride, my arrogance, my self-righteousness and my critical spirit. Painfully, as he took away those masks, I began to see myself as I really was, as he saw me – and I did not like it. Instead of looking at the speck in my brother's eye, I started to look at the log in my own eye; and I realised that, if I was really in earnest about revival, it had to begin in me. On my knees, alone before God, there was nothing I could boast about, and much of which I was frankly ashamed, although I had become skilled at hiding it from others and even from myself. I found that I was the one who was poverty-stricken, and I found this a most uncomfortable disclosure.

Blessed are those who mourn. Again, the word in the Greek is a strong word, meaning 'lament'. If I dropped a glass and it broke into many pieces, the word I would use in the Greek to describe the scene is the root word of 'mourn'. In other words, blessed are those who are shattered – why? Because of their poverty of spirit. There is natural logic in these Beatitudes: the first leads directly to the second, and so on. As I meditated on this statement by Jesus, I began literally to weep for my spiritual poverty. I saw my low level of faith, my lack of love for Jesus, the poverty of my love towards others, and it deeply concerned me. I saw that it was precisely for such sins that Jesus had been crucified on the cross, and that by my sinful attitudes I was grieving the Spirit of God. Grief is a love-word. I knew that God still loved me more than I could possibly imagine, but there was much in my life that hurt him; and the knowledge of that broke me. More deeply than I can ever remember, I began to repent of everything that I knew was wrong in my life.

Blessed are the meek. The meek person is someone who is so mourning for his spiritual poverty that he is willing for God to do what he likes in his life. That man will not protest or complain; he will not dictate his terms of reference; like the Virgin Mary he will say, 'Let it be to me according to your word.' Now that I felt broken at the foot of the cross, I was willing for God to have his own way in my life, whatever that meant, and however painful it might be. When Mary surrendered her body to become the mother of Jesus, she did not know what this would mean in later years. Simeon warned her that 'a sword will pierce through your own soul also'; and her agony when Jesus was crucified must have cut through to the innermost part of her being. There is always a price to pay for spiritual life. Many Christians want to see new life in their churches; not so many are willing to bear the cost. God brought me to that point where I was genuinely willing to say, as far as I understood it, 'Not my will, but yours be done.'

Blessed are those who hunger and thirst for righteousness. Now that I was broken at the cross, mourning for my spiritual poverty, I had a consuming desire to be right with God, to be filled with his Spirit, to glorify him in every area of my life. I spent much time in prayer, asking God to do something new in my life. Never before had I known such hunger for God. As with Jacob, I said in my heart, 'I will not let you go, unless you bless me.' Time and again I asked God specifically to fill me with his Spirit, knowing from my study of revival that the Spirit of God often revealed himself in tremendous power, falling on men and women in such a way that they were either struck to the ground or filled with 'inexpressible joy'. But as much as I was willing for anything to happen, nothing did. I was disappointed, perhaps a little disillusioned; but the hunger never abated. It may be worth adding that all this took place during the winter months of 1962–3, some time before anything was popularly known about 'charismatic renewal'. However, around that time prayer groups for revival were springing up all over the place, which I took as a mark of the

Spirit's activity. Often these would be half nights or whole
nights of prayer, such was the increasing hunger for God
among many Christians. Parallel with my own spiritual
search, I heard that my previous parish, St. Mark's, Gillingham, had been holding nights of prayer for revival; and at one
of these (I think in February 1963) those who were present
were gently aware of being filled with the Spirit. They entered
into a new experience of the love of God. Some of the
toughest of these men (and women) had fallen in love – with
Jesus. There was no doubt that God had done something new
and wonderful within the congregation; significantly, it
seemed to me, shortly after I had left the parish! My expecta-
tion that God would meet with me also began to rise.

Suddenly I realised the missing link. I had been praying
and praying to be filled with the Spirit; but when nothing
seemed to happen I assumed that my prayer had not been
answered. As I shared this with a friend, I remembered the
example of the Virgin Mary. Once she accepted God's remarkable promise to her, she began to praise God that it was
now already true, before the promise was confirmed in her
experience. I had been waiting for the experience *before* I
believed that the promise had been fulfilled. It was entirely
the wrong way round. I had to claim the promise of the Spirit,
believe it to be true, start praising God that it was true, and let
the reality or experience of the promise follow in God's own
way and in God's own time.

Once again, I confessed every sin I could think of, and
asked for God's forgiveness, even the sphere of my unbelief. I
told him that I was willing to obey him, whatever the cost. I
then asked him to fill me with his Spirit, *and began to praise
him that he had now done it*. As I went on praising for perhaps
ten or fifteen minutes, I had a quiet but overwhelming sense
of being embraced by the love of God. There were no startling
manifestations. I did not speak in tongues, and anyway I still
believed that these had died with the apostles. But it seemed
that the presence of God filled the room in which I was
praying. I *knew* I had been filled with the Spirit, and I was
bubbling over with new joy.

I went straight round to my dear friend, Dr. Basil Atkinson. 'Basil,' I said, like someone bursting with good news, 'I've been filled with the Spirit!' 'Praise the Lord!' replied Basil spontaneously, and we had a wonderful time of praise and thanksgiving together. The next day I went to a clergy meeting in Cambridge, and I said to one of them: 'Peter, I've been filled with the Spirit!' with the same exuberance I shared with Basil. Poor Peter did not know what to say. Nervously he looked out of the window. 'I think it may rain today,' was his only comment; and he moved to talk to someone else about funeral fees, or whatever was the vital business of that clergy meeting. I began to comprehend that I had to choose my moment, to speak to the right person in the right way at the right time. But God had met with me in a fresh way: of that I was certain. It was hard being silent about it.

6

Baptism or Fullness

No doubt I made many mistakes. Everyone in love tends to say and do stupid things at times. And I was in love with Jesus in a way I had never known before. I devoured the Song of Solomon, that exquisite love poem in the Old Testament, which is a beautiful analogy of a love relationship between the believer and his or her Lord. It expressed what I felt in the depths of my heart. I spent even more time in prayer, mostly praise and worship; and at times the presence of God was so real to me that I would open my eyes expecting to see him transfigured there in front of me. I read the Bible as never before, and certain passages leapt out at me as though they were alive. They all seemed like love-letters from God. In terms of personal evangelism I had never known such fruitfulness, often having the joy of leading four or five people to the Lord every week, and this lasted for months! I loved people with a new quality of love, and found many opportunities of sharing what God had done in my life, especially with those who were hungry for him.

But what exactly *had* God done in my life? The reality of it all was unmistakable and undeniable, but how could I understand it in biblical and theological terms? That was the difficulty. So began six months or more of furious study to try to grasp from the Scriptures what it was all about. With three friends I went to see a man whose ministry we immensely respected and whose concern for revival was well known, Dr. Martyn Lloyd-Jones. As we spent the day with him at Westminster Chapel, he began by asking us to share our testimonies with him, since we had all known a fresh working of the Spirit of God in our lives over the last few months. The testimonies had obvious personal variations, but were significantly the same. To our surprise, Dr. Lloyd-Jones then shared a very similar testimony of his own, when the Spirit had come upon him shortly after the Hebrides Revival in 1949, through the ministry of Duncan Campbell. He said that it had given him a new authority in his preaching ministry. As we talked a little further he said, 'Gentlemen, I believe that you have been baptized with the Holy Spirit.'

To be honest I was not happy with that expression, and to some extent have never been, if it refers to something subsequent to conversion. But the Doctor (as he was often called) was quite adamant in his preaching on this theme. Less than two years before, on May 25th, 1961, the Doctor had said this in a sermon:

> There are some who are guilty of quenching the Spirit by limiting in their very thinking the possibilities of life in the Spirit . . . I am convinced that there are large numbers of Christian people who are quenching the Spirit unconsciously by denying these possibilities in their very understanding of the doctrine of the Spirit. There is nothing, I am convinced, that so quenches the Spirit as the teaching that identifies the baptism in the Holy Ghost with regeneration. But it is a very commonly held teaching today. Indeed it has been the popular view for many years. They say that the baptism in the Spirit is 'non-experimental', that it happens to everybody at regeneration. So we say 'Ah, well, I am already baptized with the Spirit, it happened when I was born again, it happened at my conversion; I've got it all.' Got it all? I simply ask, in the name of God, why then are you as you are? If you have got it all, why are you so unlike the New Testament Christians? Got it all? Got it at your conversion! Well, where is it, I ask?

A fair question! It was one that perfectly summed up my own feelings about a shallow doctrine of assurance that all too

easily can lead to complacency. It is true that we are justified
in the sight of God the moment that we put our trust in Jesus.
But what about the 'fullness of life' that Jesus promised?
Where is the evidence of the spiritual wealth that should be
ours, as individuals and as a Church, once we are in Christ?
The renewing work of the Spirit, whatever it should be called,
seemed to be waking us up to the normal New Testament
Christian life.

For me, it was essentially an enhancement of the reality of
my spiritual life. The Doctor, while rejoicing in what God had
done, warned us of certain dangers, notably lest any doctrine
of sinless perfection should creep in. In the past, when men
and women had been blessed by the Spirit (whatever they
called it), they sometimes claimed that they were so dead to
sin and so full of love that it was no longer possible for them to
sin. When the great Baptist preacher Charles Spurgeon heard
a man teaching such nonsense at a conference one evening, he
poured a jug of milk over the man's head at breakfast the next
morning. By the man's unholy reaction, the doctrine of sinless
perfection was speedily disproved!

In my own case, the filling of the Spirit had nothing to do
with any claims to sinless perfection, but the whole spiritual
dimension had become more real. Instead of going up and
down at a fairly low level of reality, God was more real, Jesus
more real, prayer more real, the devil more real. However I
was still going up and down, albeit on this new level of reality.
I had definitely not yet arrived. I was anything but perfect.
Indeed one or two unexpected lapses into sin brought me
back with a jolt. If I had been renewed in the Spirit, I needed a
constant, daily, fresh renewal. I could take nothing for
granted.

This was a period of much heart searching, diligent study
and many meetings. Because of the growing number of
people in the country claiming to be filled or baptized with the
Spirit, John Stott was asked to produce a clear paper setting
out the biblical doctrines. This he did with his usual clarity,
authority and graciousness, but taking a view diametrically
opposed to that of Dr. Martyn Lloyd-Jones. In what became

his booklet *The Baptism and Fullness of the Holy Spirit*, John Stott said: 'According to Scripture we have been baptized with the Spirit because we have repented and believed . . . I would appeal to you not to urge upon people a baptism with the Spirit as a second and subsequent experience entirely distinct from conversion, for this cannot be proved from Scripture.' What was I to make of this 'clash of the Titans', as a friend of mine once described it? Which view was right? Had I (and others) been 'baptized in the Spirit'? If not, what had happened in our experience?

The expression 'to baptize in the Holy Spirit' comes only seven times in the New Testament, six of them linked with the baptism that John the Baptist said the Coming One would bring.[1] John had come to baptize with water as a sign of repentance, but Jesus would baptize with the Holy Spirit to introduce people into the blessings of the New Covenant. At Pentecost this promise was fulfilled, and this was repeated only in the house of Cornelius, at the Gentile equivalent of Pentecost. As Peter explained, 'And I remembered the word of the Lord, how he said, "John baptized with water, but you shall be baptized with the Holy Spirit."' Peter went on, 'God gave the same gift to them as he gave to us *when we believed in the Lord Jesus Christ*' (Acts 11:16f). Repentance (Acts 11:18; cf 2:38) and faith are thus the only necessary conditions for a person to be baptized in the Holy Spirit.

From those six references it seems clear that the baptism in the Holy Spirit refers to Christian initiation. It is the spiritual event by which all people are brought into Christ, whether Jew or Gentile. This is even more clear in the seventh reference: 'For by one Spirit we were all baptized into one body – Jews or Greeks, slaves or free – and all were made to drink of one Spirit.' (1 Cor. 12:13) Nowhere is it suggested that Christians were, or could be, baptized in the Spirit after their conversion to Christ. Indeed, 'anyone who does not have the Spirit of Christ does not belong to him' (Romans 8:9). Nor is it suggested that Christians should pray or wait for

1. Matt. 3:11; Mark 1:8; Luke 3:16; John 1:33; Acts 1:5; 11:16; 1 Cor. 12:13.

the baptism of the Spirit. The first disciples had to wait for the
initial outpouring of the Spirit at Pentecost; but after that, the
'promise of the Spirit' was for all those who repented and
believed.

The trouble about speaking of the baptism of the Holy
Spirit as a second-stage experience for some Christians (as the
Pentecostals and many charismatics do) is not only that it
cannot be proved in the New Testament, but it also becomes
divisive. The Christian Church is thus split into the haves and
have-nots, leading to inevitable dangers of spiritual arrogance
on the one hand and resistance to the Holy Spirit on the other.
The truth is that we have 'every spiritual blessing in Christ'
(Ephesians 1:3), and there is nothing further that we have to
seek beyond Christ. This is what John Stott taught so clearly.

The challenge that Dr. Martyn Lloyd-Jones made, however, was a valid and important one, even though I believe
that he was wrong to describe it as a baptism in the Spirit.
Theologically we may have everything in Christ, but where is
it in our lives? Where is the vitality and joy, the faith and love
of those first disciples? The fact is that the actual experience of
what we already have in Christ may come to different people
at different times and in different ways. It is like unwrapping a
multiple parcel, and Paul significantly talks about the 'unsearchable riches of Christ'. The truth of what we are and
have in Christ may become real in our experience at various
stages. When a person is overwhelmed by the love of Christ,
filled with new praise, and finds fresh joy in prayer, in the
study of the Scriptures and in personal witness, it is understandable if he speaks of this experience as the 'baptism of the
Spirit', even if that is not the scriptural meaning of that phrase
as we have seen.

The tragedy is that, through the unscriptural use of language, many Christians have held back from those riches in
Christ that the Holy Spirit is today renewing in the Church.
We cannot settle for a dull orthodoxy or for a low level of
spirituality. We need to be open to all that the Spirit is doing
in our midst since none of us has yet arrived. We have not yet
entered into the 'glorious liberty of the children of God'.

There is much more for all of us to experience of our inheritance in Christ, and we should always remain hungry and thirsty for him.

Most Christians would agree that we all need to be continuously filled with the Spirit, since that is the plain injunction in Scripture (Eph. 5:18). But not all Christians expect anything much to happen. Many believe and teach that it is purely a matter of 'imperceptible growth into Christ'. That is not, however, the constant testimony of countless Christians all over the world who have experienced some form of spiritual renewal, whatever it should be called. A Diocesan Youth Chaplain wrote to me,

> I was aware of the need of something more from God . . .
> One day I received the Spirit through prayer and the laying on of hands . . . I felt the Spirit pour in until it seemed I must burst . . . For how many years I had been longing for joy! And now it came, joy that welled up within and issued in praise and thanks and adoration to a glorious God. Love also began to appear . . . Christ was more real and more loved. The Scriptures came alive in a new way . . .

That man has developed a powerful and gracious ministry since then; and such stories could be multiplied many hundreds of thousands of times.

Something happens, therefore, when men and women are filled with the Spirit, and that 'something' can often transform a person's life and ministry. Whole churches come alive in a way not known before. If the expression 'to baptize with the Spirit' should be kept for the initiation into Christ, this must not exclude the serious possibility of further significant steps forward that are variously termed 'being filled with the Spirit', 'receiving the Spirit', or 'experiencing the release of the Spirit'. In our Western Christianity we have become so cautious about subjective experiences because of their obvious dangers that we tend to rule them out altogether. However, no one can read the New Testament without seeing that it is shot through with specific and often dramatic experiences of the Spirit. It is because of the comparative absence of these that the Church today stands in such desperate need of renewal. Although it is important to get our terminology right, it is tragic if we allow our debates about terminology to stifle our hunger for God and our openness to the Spirit.

At the same time as Dr. Martyn Lloyd-Jones and John Stott were expounding their different viewpoints, news was coming through from North America of Episcopal and Lutheran churches that were in a similar way being renewed in the Spirit, although most of them testified to speaking in tongues (a love-language of praise in the Spirit) which had not been my experience at all. Several interested Christian leaders met in London with those who came over from North America to share their stories with us. Some of them, to be honest, impressed us very little. We sensed that they had simply been 'born again', and their abundance of stories and absence of theology left us far from satisfied. Others were more impressive, and certainly something seemed to be happening; but whether it was genuinely a work of the Spirit or some Satanic diversion from the true heart of the Gospel was not always easy to discern. One man, at an extravagant luncheon for Christian leaders at the Hilton Hotel, was introduced as 'the greatest Spirit-filled Christian in the world today' (applause for the platform party). This did not go down too well with us conservative English clergy. It was a puzzling period in our lives.

In particular, there was this new emphasis on tongues, together with some reference to prophecy and healing. During my theological studies I had become a 'dispensationalist', following the teaching of such men as B. B. Warfield, believing that all such gifts, whatever they were, were purely for the New Testament period, to establish the truth of the Gospel with 'many wonders and signs', but definitely not for today. However, at a conference for evangelical clergy some months before, I had heard Dr. Edwin Orr speak on his specialised subject of revival. It was a fascinating day, and he made one statement in particular that I remembered. Tracing quickly through history, he pointed out that each significant revival within the Church had brought back something lost since the days of the early Church. He also predicted that the next revival would bring back certain gifts of the Spirit that had largely disappeared since the first few centuries of church history. Was this what God had been doing through the Pentecostal movement since the turn of the century? Was this what he was beginning to do again, attempting once more to break into the historic denominations which had unitedly rejected those gifts earlier, thus forcing the Pentecostal Church to come into being? What was the scriptural teaching about those gifts? Were they really for today after all?

The more I studied the New Testament the more I became convinced: the teaching that these gifts were only for the apostolic age was no more than a rationalisation of their absence for so long. The arguments against them were thin and questionable; I could see that all the gifts could be just as edifying for the Church today as in the first century, and many of them just as effective for the evangelistic thrust of the Church today as in the Acts of the Apostles. Granted that there was a 'foundational' level of prophecy for the completion of Scripture (and therefore not to be looked for today), even in the New Testament Church there were many other levels of prophecy for the building up of believers; so why not today? I could not readily understand the value of tongues, except that, especially with my new longing to worship and praise the Lord, I often felt frustrated by the limitations of language. My spirit often wished to transcend my ability to express myself in grammatical sentences. This was equally true for intercession when I did not know exactly what to pray for, but felt a strong burden to pray for someone.

Such thoughts developed in my mind over a period of about six months, by which time I had started 'earnestly to desire spiritual gifts', according to the command in Scripture. At one time a dear couple laid hands on me and prayed for me for a whole hour, asking that I would be given the gift of tongues. For the first five minutes I prayed with them. For the next five I could only think, 'What *would* some of my colleagues say if they could see me now?' And then for the next fifty minutes I prayed that they would stop praying. Eventually I won, and the whole experience was not particularly helpful for me. I suppose I was expecting God to waggle my tongue so that the words would rush out. But it never happened to me like that. Later I was impressed by Luke's statement in Acts 2:4 that '*they* . . . began to speak in other tongues, as the Spirit gave them utterance.' They had to do the speaking. The Spirit does not normally take us over in the way in which an evil spirit may do.

So eventually I asked God to give me a language in the Spirit through which I could worship and praise him. I began to praise him in English, and then let my mind relax while my spirit went on praising with the first syllables that came to my tongue. They could be any syllables; there was nothing special or mystical about them. After some thirty seconds I stopped: 'David, you're just making this up!' I said to myself. Then I thought, what if God had answered my prayer? What if I had been speaking in tongues? At the very least I should go on for a little longer. I was sure that God would not be angry with me if I were doing the wrong thing. He knew that I genuinely wanted to praise him as much as I could. So I went on making these noises for about thirty minutes or more. Every time I listened carefully to the sounds, I found them most unedifying. But every time I used the sounds to concentrate on the Lord in worship, I found myself unusually refreshed. Is this what Paul meant when he wrote, 'He who speaks in a tongue edifies himself'? I cannot pretend that all my problems about tongues were solved from that moment onwards. I was deeply concerned about the integrity of what I was doing, and I wanted to be *sure*. But increasingly I found the gift to be a natural and helpful part of my daily devotional prayer life – a marvellous way of abiding and resting in the Lord.

All language is simply the use of various sounds or syllables as vehicles of communication. When my spirit is praying to God, who is Spirit, I need not be confined to those sounds that happen to form my native language. Any sounds or syllables will do, providing that they are genuinely vehicles of communication between my spirit and God's Spirit. Of course in public I must use sounds that everyone understands. But in private that need not be the case. Every Christian acknowledges the importance of silent prayer, or 'sighs too deep for words'. Why not a spiritual language which the mind may not understand? Tongues are not irrational, but 'trans-rational' or supra-rational. God is so much bigger than our own rational thinking. Therefore, Paul concludes, 'I will pray with the spirit (i.e. in tongues) and I will pray with the mind also (i.e. in a known language); I will sing with the spirit and I will sing with the mind also' (1 Cor. 14:15).

Because of the novelty of all this, I kept very quiet about it and told only a tiny handful of friends in strict confidence, that I thought I was beginning to speak in tongues in private prayer. I was living at a Biblical Research Centre at the time, and such news could easily be misunderstood. Imagine my concern, therefore, when I was suddenly asked to leave the Centre and find other accommodation. When I made a direct enquiry about the reason for this, I was told that the committee responsible for the Centre had heard that I was speaking in tongues. This threw me into a dilemma. Was I becoming heretical? Was all this a deception of the devil? Was I in danger of leading others astray if I spoke openly about this? To whom could I turn for wise counsel? It was not an easy period in my life, to say the least; and once more I had to go back to the New Testament to gain a better understanding of the nature and value of spiritual gifts. However, the gift of tongues was constantly refreshing whenever I used it as a genuine prayer language for the Lord.

As I found myself unexpectedly homeless, Mark Ruston graciously took me in, and I tried to continue working in the church much as before. I was anxious to be utterly loyal to Mark and to the ministry of that church, and yet I naturally longed to share something about the renewing work of the Spirit that I had experienced. Obviously I would say nothing about tongues or any of the other controversial gifts. So I continued running the Children's Church, which had been my special and enjoyable responsibility, I continued preaching at the normal services, and I began to become more involved in the work among students. Whatever private misgivings Mark may have had, I have always respected him for his patient and steady acceptance of me as a person, and our relationship over the years is something I have always treasured.

Nevertheless, in the country as a whole during the sixties there was growing opposition by a number of evangelical leaders towards this renewal movement. Various well-known leaders wrote to me, urging me to 'renounce tongues'. One man even offered me a 'plum living' in the south of England if I would make a simple but clean break from all these things. But if I had received a genuine gift from the Holy Spirit of God, how could I possibly renounce it? Would I not be opposing God and quenching his Spirit? Risking the accusation of arrogance, I knew that I must obey God rather than men, although I went over the biblical ground for my new convictions again and again. A number of letters that I received hurt me deeply.

The heart-searching continued. I did not *know* I was right. Perhaps I was all wrong and my critics were right after all. But I knew it could never be right to go against one's own conscience. All I could do was to commit the whole matter to God and ask him to lead me in his way, whatever the cost might be.

I also found that another form of heart-searching was beginning to develop which took me equally by surprise.

7

Marriage

It was Christmas Day 1963. The Christmas morning service
had just finished, and I was standing with Mark Ruston at the
Norman porch of the Round Church saying 'Happy Christmas' to all the members of the congregation. A very attractive
girl suddenly caught my eye. 'Have we met before?' I asked. 'I
don't think so,' she replied with a trace of a Scottish accent.
'My name is Anne MacEwan Smith, and I'm nursing at the
Maternity Hospital in Mill Lane.'

I had always mistrusted the romantic sentiment of 'love at
first sight', but the 'vibes' were undoubtedly there. A little
later, driving from Cambridge to my mother's home in East-
bourne, I could think of little else all the way except Anne
MacEwan Smith. That brief encounter had made a deep
impression on me.

Since my conversion I had considered carefully the advantages of the celibate life. The apostle Paul was strong on this
theme: 'I want you to be free from anxieties. The unmarried
man is anxious about the affairs of the Lord, how to please the
Lord; but the married man is anxious about worldly affairs,
how to please his wife' (1 Cor. 7:32). I was now thirty, and
since my conversion over nine years ago I had devoted most of
my time and energy to the work of Christ. David MacInnes
and I had often discussed the matter, and we could think of
very few advantages in getting married. We were confirmed
bachelors, so I thought. And I believed that a bachelor was a
man who never made the same mistake once.

Two facts weakened my resolve, however. The first was

that David himself became engaged! I felt almost betrayed,
and yet secretly happy for him, and gladly accepted his
invitation to be his Best Man. The second fact was that, to my
surprise, I now wanted to get married myself. The time
seemed right.

I tried not to think too much of Anne MacEwan Smith in
the next few weeks, and in fact I forgot her name (but not her
face!) when we next met at a church meeting. I did not plan to
rush into things, and I gather that she had the same idea.
Brought up as a good Scottish Presbyterian, but living now in
England and going mostly to Anglican churches, she felt that
she ought to be confirmed in the Church of England. Dutifully
and discreetly she approached my vicar, Mark Ruston, and
asked if he could prepare her for confirmation. 'You must see
my curate,' was his reply. 'I am shortly going on a three-
month sabbatical.' She obeyed his instructions and came over
to see me.

I had in fact already started the confirmation classes, and
since we were covering a carefully planned syllabus, it was
necessary for Anne to catch up on the classes she had missed.
Whether it was appropriate or not, I arranged to give her one
or two private classes before she could join the rest. At our
first session I handed her an Anglican Prayer Book and asked
her to turn to the Confirmation Service. Following my usual
practice, I commented, 'You will find it just before the
marriage service!' A word of prophecy indeed!

Correctly we covered the ground that she had missed, but
gently I also asked her a few questions about her own
relationship with Christ. She had always been God-fearing,
but had personally accepted Christ as her Saviour only two or
three years before while training at Guy's Hospital. I asked
her if she knew what it meant to be filled with the Holy Spirit,
and when her reply was a little evasive I gave her a booklet on
the subject which I had found helpful.

The next week she explained that the booklet had clarified
a remarkable spiritual experience that she had recently
known. Apparently she had been reading an article from a
missionary magazine which challenged her about her own

lack of faith. On her knees, alone before God, she asked him to give her a gift of faith. In answer to her prayer it seemed that the Spirit had fallen on her and she was caught up into God's presence, losing all sense of time. When she became more aware of everything around her, she heard a strange sound and found that she was praising God in a tongue that was foreign to her. She had never heard of speaking in tongues, and feared that she might be going out of her mind. But she continued secretly to use this language because through it she experienced the presence and love of Jesus more than ever before. However, having read the booklet that I gave her, she shared her story with me. I marvelled that, despite the difference of our two stories, the end result was the same. With me, it had been a long, tortuous struggle, filled with intellectual questionings and many doubts. With Anne, it had been a sovereign work of the Spirit of God, without her knowing anything about spiritual renewal or spiritual gifts. As far as I could see, her experience was wholly authentic, and she evidently had a deep love for Jesus. It was probably at this point that my instinctive interest in Anne began to deepen. That increased when I first heard her pray in a prayer meeting. It was a heartfelt prayer which flowed with amazing spiritual authority, vision and understanding. I had already been physically attracted to her, but I felt even more at one with her when we were both on our knees before God; and this, for me, was enormously important. If God were to bless my future relationship, I knew that Christ must unquestionably be first. Indeed, the quality of our individual relationships with Christ would determine the quality of our relationship together. If we were not first and foremost 'one in Christ', I could see no future for us as a couple. It was therefore marvellous to feel so close to Anne in prayer.

We soon became aware of our mutual affection, but recognised the extreme difficulty of pursuing this when I was the curate of the Round Church. A bachelor curate has no privacy when it comes to personal friendships with the opposite sex, especially if the girl is a member of his own congregation. A period of essential subterfuge followed. We knew that we could not be seen together in Cambridge – the news would travel everywhere within minutes – so we planned our free time very carefully. Sometimes I would sit in my car outside the Maternity Hospital, complete with slouched hat and dark glasses, hiding carefully behind a copy of *The Times*. I could well be tracking down the Pink Panther! On other days, Anne would take a bus to some prearranged place several miles out of Cambridge, and I would follow the bus in my car at a discreet distance. I am not sure what the bus driver thought when I stopped every time the bus stopped, but the plan always worked. With this skilful cloak-and-dagger courtship we arrived at the point of announcing our engagement without anyone knowing about it, except for a very small circle whom we had told in confidence. The announcement stunned many in the congregation, but they shared in our joy. We planned to get married in the Round Church on September 19th.

I was as happy as could be! God had blessed me spiritually, and now had given me a beautiful fiancée who had also experienced spiritual renewal.

As the wedding drew near, however, totally unexpected and serious problems arose. During the month before our wedding I was involved in some Christian activity, and an incident occurred which, although slight in itself, seemed to oppose all the new-found joy and freedom in worship that had become so important to me. I felt a deep grief within my own spirit, and sensed that this was only a pale reflection of the much more serious grief of the Spirit of God. Whether or not I was right about this, I suddenly felt in a spiritual strait-jacket. At that moment I experienced something like a steel band tightening round my chest, and I began coughing. That night I continued coughing, and it steadily grew worse so that sleep became more and more difficult. I went to a local doctor who was puzzled. But by this time I was clearly so breathless and ill that Anne was sent for to take me to her parents' home. As the shortness of breath grew more acute I became quite fearful at night and was obviously far from well. The wedding was only three weeks away.

When I returned to Cambridge I was so short of breath that I could not perform the simplest task requiring any effort. Even walking down a street was a major achievement. My doctor diagnosed some form of bronchial asthma, but the treatment in those days was rather a hit-and-miss affair compared with the efficient treatment that asthma sufferers can receive today. On the eve of our wedding I was so ill that Anne seriously suggested that we should postpone the whole affair until I was better. Perhaps we should have done so, but with 250 guests arriving from all over the country the next morning the suggestion seemed impossible. So, supported by drugs, I struggled through the service and endured the reception. At one level I was blissfully happy to have Anne as my bride. But physically I was distressed and mentally anxious. Doubtless Anne was exceedingly worried too.

Our honeymoon was really a disaster. We went to a beautiful spot in North Cornwall, Trebarwith Strand, which we had carefully selected some months before. When we arrived there, we were almost the only ones in a delightful hotel, and the weather for two weeks was absolutely perfect: blue skies, glorious sunshine, fantastic waves for surfing – it could not have been better. Except that I could not breathe! Each night was constantly interrupted by coughing; each day saw a brief struggle to a spot within fifty yards of the hotel, where we had to stay all day, reading, talking, coughing and attempting to sleep. We never went as far as the beach. We never went for one walk.

The nightmare continued on our return to Cambridge. We had rented a small flat, but climbing even one flight of stairs proved an impossible task for me on some days. Anne had planned to go back to nursing to help out financially, but through an amazingly generous gift from a friend (who did not know our situation intimately), no job was necessary and Anne did her 'nursing' instead at home.

We tried to enter into the work together, but this too was fraught with problems. Without realising at all what I was doing, I made a series of disastrous mistakes. To begin with I attempted to make Anne into a mini-evangelist overnight, giving her a crash-course in personal evangelism, and I could not understand why she rebelled so strongly against this. It seemed to me that she was not interested in trying to bring people to Christ, and, since that was my primary calling, how could our marriage possibly work out? I failed to appreciate the importance of Paul's comment that only '*some* are evangelists'. I was; but Anne wasn't. In fact God has given her many spiritual gifts which have blessed countless people over the years, but it took me a long time to recognise the fact that God had planned that our gifts and ministries should be complementary and not identical.

The next mistake came when I tried to mould Anne into the conventional clergyman's wife: a sort of unpaid curate whose job was to support *me* in *my* ministry. This meant, in part, constant hospitality in our flat, which for Anne was far from easy. In our own living room, which was also my study, half the furniture had to be moved every time we entertained anyone for a meal; and anyway nearly all those who came were *my* friends and *my* contacts, not Anne's. 'Supporting me' also meant that I took her with me to meetings and conferences at which I was the speaker, so that everyone knew at once who she was, 'David's wife'. Anne, on her part, knew very few of those present and even began to lose her own identity. Who was she? Was she no more than 'David's wife'? What was her role now that she was married? Was she just an addition to me, like another suitcase that I was carrying around? Who was Anne Watson? In marriage we are called to lose our independence but not our individuality.

None of this did I understand. Even if Anne had articulated the problem to me clearly, I doubt if I would have grasped what she was talking about. As it was, her defence was to withdraw into herself, often curling up on the bed in depressed silence. When I asked what was the matter, she did not answer. When I mentioned that it was time for us to go to this meeting or to that house, often she did not come. Many times during those first few months I had to make the same apology: 'I'm sorry that Anne isn't with me, but she's not too well.' Outwardly I made light of it, but inwardly I was extremely worried. With the hectic pace we were trying to keep up (far from successfully) it was not surprising that Anne had a miscarriage. Mentally and physically we were exhausted, and that in itself is a reason why some marriages flounder from the start. Space needs to be given for mutual adjustment, but these were lessons that we learnt only when it was too late.

We never forgot, however, an incredible sky that we saw on our way to Cornwall for our honeymoon. It was a striking mixture of black, grey and a violent orangey-yellow – an astonishing blend of storm and sunset. And boldly sweeping across the whole scene, in the most vivid colours imaginable, was a *double rainbow*. Had a painter depicted the scene accurately on canvas I would have said it was far too lurid to be true. But it was there before our startled eyes. God, many years before, had set a rainbow in the sky as a sign of his covenant promises. It seemed to us, in that double rainbow before us, that God was giving us a double assurance of his love, whatever storms there might be in the future. Even after such a desperate start to our marriage, we did not realise how much we would need that assurance in the years that lay ahead.

8

St. Cuthbert's, York – Early Days

'What are we going to do with you when we close you down?'
This was the discouraging and unnerving question that I was
asked on my second full day in St. Cuthbert's Church, York.
The questioner was the Chairman of the Church Redundancy
Commission who had come with the rest of the Commission
to consider the future use of the church building. I had only
just arrived, believing that it had a future as a living church;
the Commission were already planning its future as a possible
museum for York University. What a marvellous welcome to
receive, I thought to myself! And what a parable of the
popular image of the Church in the mid-sixties: a museum, an
ancient relic of some bygone days, of occasional interest to
historians and architects but of absolutely no relevance for the
mass of ordinary people. I gave the Chairman what may have
seemed a typically pious remark from a young clergyman: 'If
anyone comes to this church and preaches the simple Gospel
of Christ, believes in the power of prayer and trusts in the
Holy Spirit, this building will be full in no time.' Uncon-
vinced, they gave me one year's grace before, regretfully,
they would have to close St. Cuthbert's down.

Although it was purely a matter of faith, Anne and I were
convinced that God had called us to York. When we knew
that our time in Cambridge was coming to an end, we were
offered four livings, each of which presented a reasonable
salary and a good vicarage. After my happy experience in
Gillingham we were particularly interested in a church in the
East End of London, but I felt that a new pastoral scheme,

attempting to unite two parishes that were totally divided by a huge railway cutting, would never work, so we turned the offer down.

Then someone mentioned this little church in York. Having seen the valuable supporting ministry to students that the Round Church played in Cambridge, I was concerned for the new universities that were springing up throughout the country, most of them thoroughly secular in their foundation. I could see that they needed, far more than Oxford and Cambridge, local churches that were relevant to students. York University had only recently started, with 600 students, and no church in York had obvious potential to play this supportive role. As a few Christians in York were praying about this, the idea of St. Cuthbert's Church came to their minds.

St. Cuthbert's had been increasingly run down for many years. Much of the parish had disappeared through a slum-clearance programme, and in the place of the rabbit warrens of tiny houses, light industry was beginning to emerge. The previous rector of St. Cuthbert's, the Rev. R. V. Bainton, had been at the church for twenty-four years, but had suffered from poor eyesight and was totally blind for the last years of his ministry, which ended in a tragic death early in 1964. The tiny congregation nobly soldiered on, and the parish was annexed to Heworth Parish Church, a mile away, to maintain the necessary services. The total Sunday offerings each week averaged about £2, and the majority of the year's income came through jumble sales, garden parties, whist drives and raffles. In this way the church itself was just solvent, but the fourteen-roomed Victorian rectory was cold, damp, dirty and in urgent need of complete redecoration. The congregation had dwindled to about four or five for the eight o'clock Communion Service, the same for Mattins, and ten or twelve for Evensong. That they stayed there at all was perhaps remarkable, but the future of the church was undoubtedly bleak.

Added to that, when Anne and I first visited York to consider the situation, we arrived on an exceptionally foggy day; and any sufferer will know that fog is not the best weather for asthma. I noticed that not only was the rectory cold and damp, with no form of heating apart from open coal fires in every room right up to the 'servants' quarters' on the third floor, but the church was heated by two coke stoves whose fumes, I was told, could be lethal when the wind was in the wrong direction. With the fog alone (we were given warm hospitality in someone's home), my asthma was so bad that I had to spend the whole night upright in an armchair, as I coughed ceaselessly whenever I tried to lie down. It was one of many similar nights that I was to experience in the coming months.

Other prospects also were bleak. With the expected closure of the church within the year, the Church Commissioners understandably decided that they would not spend any money on the rectory at all, apart from any essential repairs. The house was re-wired, admittedly, but we found only one socket in each of the huge rooms, and hard lumps of dried plaster all over the dirty floorboards. Also, with the church annexed to Holy Trinity, Heworth, I would not be appointed as rector of St. Cuthbert's, but licensed as curate to Holy Trinity, with responsibility for St. Cuthbert's. My salary in Cambridge, when Anne and I were living in a small furnished flat, had been £900 a year, and that had been inadequate until the generous gift from my friend arrived which effectively raised it to over £1200. Now we were to move to a filthy, cold, unfurnished fourteen-roomed house, and my salary dropped to £600 a year – a figure, I suspect, well below the poverty-line. One or two clerical friends expressed concern about this, but nothing, apparently, could be done. Indeed, out of that £600 we had to buy two night-storage heaters to try to warm a part of the rectory, pay for all removal expenses from Cambridge, purchase a duplicator for the parish, and scavenge as much second-hand furniture as we could. My parents-in-law advanced their 'will' to us, enabling us to buy some carpets and curtains; my mother moved from a house to a flat, giving us what she no longer needed; Mark Ruston's mother did something similar; old family portraits, trunks and packing cases were released from storage by my uncle; and when families living near us in York were buying new pieces of furniture (sofas and armchairs for example) we would gratefully take their throw-outs from them. In this way, the fourteen rooms were gradually furnished, if not exactly to our taste!

Why did we ever go to such an unpromising parish? We were warned that York would be something of a backwater for us. We had already heard about the 'spiritual barrenness' of the north-east, where few churches of any denomination showed signs of spiritual life, but we had no idea how desperately barren it was until we moved there. We were told by several Christians in York that the city was such a tough place as far as the Gospel was concerned that we would lose our spiritual cutting-edge within three years, if we did not watch out. We had no personal links in York; and all that we knew about the city was its Minster, its railways and two famous chocolate factories. So why did we go?

We went because we believed, deeply within our hearts, that God had called us there. I am not a great one for visions and revelations, and have always been impatient with those who say, perhaps a little glibly at times, that the Lord has told them to do this or that. Anne and I prayed carefully about the five parishes that were tentatively being offered to us, and although every human consideration about York seemed totally negative, nevertheless on our knees before God the strong conviction was gaining on us that the Lord wanted us there. In fact he gave us a promise (and I'm not a great one for being given promises, either): 'I will fill this house with glory' (Hag. 2:7, A.V.). Clinging to that promise, at times by our fingernails, we moved to York on July 1st, 1965.

Our first task was to make at least one or two rooms in the rectory habitable. I had never decorated a room in my life; but fortunately Anne had some experience, and with the skilled help of a friend we decorated my study and an upstairs sitting-room within two weeks. After that, the pace slowed down considerably, and it was literally years before we got around to some parts of the house.

Nevertheless, we found the tiny congregation very welcoming, and we began to form deep friendships which have continued and grown ever since. Most of them were Linfoots: Dan Linfoot (the church-warden), Florrie Linfoot, Barbara Linfoot, Harry Linfoot, Ethel Linfoot, Doreen Linfoot, Michael Linfoot, Ethel Linfoot – when in doubt I said 'Linfoot'! Then there was Mrs. Lunn, Mr. and Mrs. Eddie Barrett, Mr. and Mrs. Brown, Mr. and Mrs. Lancaster – they were all the salt of the earth. But there were not many of them. Naturally we visited in the parish as we tried to establish relationships and tell people about the love of Jesus. Yorkshire people are blunt but friendly, although virtually no one understood why we were visiting. Some assumed it must be for money ('The Church is always asking for money'), and a few gave us £1 which they hoped would encourage us. But we wanted them to hear about God's free gift to them of his own Son, Jesus Christ. None seemed interested, and as far as I know no one came to our services as a result of our visiting.

Preaching also was initially a great strain. I prepared my sermons as thoroughly as I could and tried to deliver them with spirit – whether mine or God's, I am not sure. However, the moment I stepped into the pulpit I could see that the congregation mostly switched off; they had just done their bit, with the hymns and psalms, and it was now the clergyman's turn to do his. It was obvious that, with rare exceptions, they simply were not listening. I thought of that jingle:

> The colour of our curate's eyes
>   I cannot well define;
> For when he prays, he closes his;
>   And when he preaches, I close mine.

One of my first series of sermons was 'Abraham, a Man of Faith'. If anyone at St. Cuthbert's needed the faith of Abraham, I certainly did. So I could not wait to hear my next week's sermon! I believe, however, that God's word is always powerful; and it was a joy, over the months, to see the hearts of some within the congregation opening up to God as a flower opens to the sun. A few, I discovered later, had probably found a living faith in Christ many years before, largely through the ministry of the York City Missioner, but had been in deep-freeze for a long time. They had to be brought out of that deep-freeze and given time to thaw before their faith came to life again. Others had never understood the Gospel of Christ. One or two, inevitably, did not want it or could not accept it, and eventually left; but others slowly – very slowly – found the light of Christ penetrating the darkness within them, and they became fine Christians, a vital core of the congregation for many years to come. As in Gillingham and Cambridge, we saw the power of the Gospel of Christ to change the hearts of individuals, even if we had to learn the New Testament truth, that faith and patience go hand in hand.

Anne and I knew, of course, that if God were to do anything among us, time must be given to serious prayer. On my first Sunday I announced that there would be a short meeting for Bible study and prayer at the rectory on Thursday. It was to be held in my study, the one room we had so far decorated. About four or five turned up, one woman with her dog, and to begin with there was no great promise of revival. After giving a short and simple Bible study, I encouraged everyone to pray a few short prayers, and mentioned some needs. I prayed, and there was a long pause; Anne prayed, and there was another long pause. I prayed again, and Anne prayed again. So we all said the Grace and went home. Yet, from those slender beginnings, our Thursday Fellowship became quite the most important event in our church life, without which the Sunday services and everything else would have lacked the vitality of the Holy Spirit. Repeatedly I emphasised to the congregation the absolute importance of those corporate times of study and prayer, and the response eventually was tremendous.

To begin with, however, nothing much seemed to be happening in the parish, and Anne and I felt that God was calling us to a more sustained time of prayer. We had no children at that time, and there were very few meetings, so it was easy for us to do something about it. Every Wednesday we spent most of the day in prayer and fasting as we worshipped God, reading the Scriptures together, praying about everything in the parish, and asking for God's guidance. We knew that in any church there are always 101 good things one can do. But what was God wanting us to do in our church at that time? We kept up those days of prayer for the best part of a year; and during that year, most of the significant developments in the church came from those days. Through them we gained a sense of God's direction for his work.

One immediate concern, of course, was the matter of giving. At my first Church Council Meeting, someone asked if we could hold a Gift Day, to which I responded warmly, saying that I would be in church all day and would ask people to spend a few moments praying as well as giving. Some of the Church Council members, however, thought quite differently. They said that people would be too busy on a Saturday to come into church to pray, with all the weekend shopping to be done; but if I were to stand in my cassock outside the bus-stop near our church shaking a tin in my hand, a few coins might be given. As another suggestion, we could even string a big sheet between two trees, and passers-by could toss a coin or two into it. We might get several pounds that way.

It was, I think, the only time that I resolutely refused to do what the Church Council proposed. I insisted on being in church, inviting people to pray as well as give, and if they were too busy to say even a short prayer I was not very interested in their gifts. God looks first and foremost for the love of our hearts, not the offer of money. If the gift of money, or anything else for that matter, is a genuine expression of our love and thanksgiving to the Lord, it becomes a part of the worship that glorifies him. But nothing can be a substitute for that love-relationship that God wants us to enjoy with him in Jesus Christ.

The Council eventually acquiesced to my ideas after a brief struggle. I do not think that any previous Gift Day had yielded more than about £13. This one yielded £81 which, for that tiny and dispirited congregation, was astronomical! Over the years we never had appeals, and the jumble sales and whist

drives soon died a natural death. Each year, on the Sunday
before Harvest Thanksgiving, I would preach from the Bible
about the principles of giving. The following Friday we would
have a special time of prayer, often a half-night of prayer (as
well as the Thursday Fellowship), and on both the Saturday
and the Sunday people would come with their thank-offerings
to the Lord. The following year the total was £214, then £300;
£411; £925; £1,037; £1,120; £1,590; £2,115; £3,701; £4,154;
£5,109, and so forth. All these were specifically for missionary
support, not for the work in York. Throughout the years the
weekly offerings steadily rose too, and there were occasional
extra Gift Days to meet special expenses caused by the
expanding work. The offerings were never what they could or
should have been, but the giving of any church is a fair
barometer of the spiritual state of that church, a clear evidence of the grace of God flowing among his people. We had
much to encourage us, although nothing to leave us com-
placent.

   The first visible breakthrough in the Sunday services came
after six months when we held a monthly Family Service in the
place of traditional Mattins, and three months later this
became our weekly morning service. I had been impressed by
the value of family services both in Gillingham and Cambridge, and felt that St. Cuthbert's could benefit from a
similar approach. The Family Service is not just a children's
service. It is for the whole family, although children play an
active part by reading the lesson, helping with the offering,
and (a few years later) playing in the orchestra, praying the
prayers with the rest of their family, or taking part in a dance,
mime or piece of drama. The talks likewise are simple and
always with visual aids of one form or another, which hold the
attention of all but the youngest children and usually get
through to the parents, often with much greater clarity and
force than most conventional sermons! The philosophy behind the Family Service is also important. Whereas with the
Sunday School one part of the aim is to reach the parents
through the children (in practice this very seldom happens,
with a huge fall-away of children from the church during the

teenage years) with the Family Service the aim is to reach the
children through the parents. Thus although many parts of
the service are designed with the children in mind, we have
always found this service one of the best ways of winning
parents for Christ; and once they become Christians there is
much more chance of helping the children through that
rebellious and questioning teenage phase. We were un-
ashamedly out to see whole families brought to Christ, not
just individual boys and girls. With the Family Service, too, in
contrast to the Sunday School, children begin to feel a part of
the wider family of God's people from a very early age.
Children are as much a vital part of the family of God as
anyone else, though still young and immature, and need to be
welcomed as such.

As soon as the Family Service started we saw many encouragements. At one level, when the first new family joined
us, the congregation immediately doubled! With each new
family, the growth was excitingly visible. Seventeen years
later, the Family Service has naturally developed in various
ways, but all through the years it has been a marvellous family
occasion which appeals to almost all ages and backgrounds.
Countless visitors to the church, especially those from overseas, used to comment that they had never seen anything like
it, and were clearly deeply moved by the whole service.
Occasionally it could be noisy, but we always had a crèche
where little children could be taken at any time, so that others
could more easily concentrate on this family act of worship.

The development of any church, however, is far from easy.
Traditionally, at least within the Anglican circles, most
church-goers regard the church as a club: it is there for the
convenience of its members whenever they want to go, but
few expect to take a very active part. Most clergy have sadly
perpetuated this distortion of the nature of the church. But in
the New Testament Church every person, as a member of the
Body of Christ, played an indispensable part. With our traditional Anglican heritage, Anne and I began by doing almost
everything ourselves. We did have two marvellous weeks in
the spring of 1966 decorating the whole church, when many

people joined in, and it was like a mission to the congregation:
it brought us much closer together. But, apart from that,
Anne and I gave all our time and energy to try to build a firm
foundation for the future.

The congregation started to grow. After about eight
months the local press cautiously commented that 'there was
a reasonable chance that St. Cuthbert's would continue,
according to a member of the Archbishop of York's Commission on Redundant Churches.' Replying to this I said in my
newsletter, 'We praise God that if the Redundancy Commission came to our church on some Sunday nights, they would
be hard pressed to find a seat.' We were once picketed by
some York University students, protesting about the waste of
these empty, redundant church buildings. I noticed that the
students engaged in the protest were a little surprised to see
streams of families coming into St. Cuthbert's, and when we
invited the pickets to join us for the service we had to find
extra chairs for them since all the others were occupied!

In January 1966 another major sphere of work for me
began to open up: I led my first university mission, at Reading. For twenty-five years successive student committees at
Reading had discussed the possibility of a mission, and eventually they decided to hold one. I assumed that by the time they
had made their initial plans all the well-known speakers were
booked up, so they stumbled on me. The team working with
me were equally inexperienced and nervous, and I could see
at the pre-mission houseparty that something had to happen if
the mission were to make any impact at all. At that houseparty I spoke on the nature of faith and the vital importance
of being filled with the Holy Spirit if we were to be effective as
witnesses to Christ. I then asked everyone to go back to their
rooms and for the next half-hour to seek the power of the
Spirit in their own lives. During that half-hour God met with
many of the students in a gentle but unmistakable way, and
from that moment onwards they went into the mission full of
boldness and faith. There were only fifty members in the
Christian Union, but with daring faith they put out 120 chairs
for the first evening's meeting. Over 300 turned up, and

twelve gave their lives to Christ that night. For six nights the
mission continued like this, and by the end of the time at least
sixty students had found Christ, most of them standing firm as
Christians in the months and years ahead. Proportionately
it was probably the most fruitful of the eighty or so university missions that I have had the privilege of leading since
then.

The cost of these developments in personal terms, however, proved considerable. In our first few months in York
Anne suffered a long and deep depression, once again with-
drawing into herself and often sleeping for twelve hours or
more each night. Whatever were the basic reasons for this
depression (exhaustion doubtless being one of them), it was
only through a time of prayer and ministry by Michael and
Jeanne Harper and others, that the depression was lifted and
she was again free.

I, too, had my own problems. Wonderfully I had received a
temporary healing from asthma shortly before moving to
York. Anne and I had been at a gathering of friends at
Gillingham where a remarkable person called Edgar Trout
had been ministering. Although some of his work was un-
orthodox, the power of God was manifestly with him. This
gathering of friends unexpectedly turned into a whole night of
prayer. During it I was coughing away as usual, and so Edgar
decided to anoint me with oil and asked everyone to pray for
me. This they all did, and then started to praise God that he
had answered their prayer for healing. It was all very fine for
them, I thought to myself. They were having a great time of
praise, but I was still coughing miserably. It is easy to thank
God for healing when you do not have the affliction yourself!
At about eight in the morning Anne and I tumbled into bed
for a couple of hours, feeling a little discouraged by the night's
work, but when I woke up and got dressed I realised that I was
no longer coughing. I could walk down the street, even run up
the stairs, and still not cough. Thus healed, I was able to enter
into all the strenuous work at York without the affliction of
asthma.

After the first nine months of demanding physical, mental

and spiritual work, however, the asthma started to return with some severity. It was an extraordinarily worrying time for us both. With the strain of getting the work going in York our relationship had often been tense. We did not really understand each other, since we thought and reacted in such different ways.

It was into that stressful atmosphere that our first child, Fiona, was born, on August 10th, 1966. My attitude then towards family life, and its relation to church work, was typified by my first visit to hospital after Fiona's birth. It was a brief visit, when I hope I said and did all the right things, prayed a short prayer of thanksgiving, patted Fiona gently on the head, gave Anne a little kiss, and then rushed off to lead our Parish Fellowship. 'First things first' had always been my unspoken motto; and for me, at that time and for many years to come, the work of the church came unquestionably before my responsibilities to my family. Since I hardly knew my father before he died, I understood little about fatherhood, and I fear that I have frequently been a poor husband and a worse father. Although Fiona at once brought us a tremendous amount of joy, her arrival caused endless broken nights for nine months or more, which brought Anne to exhaustion once again. This in turn increased my asthma, and (as I saw it) the rapidly growing work of the church was hindered. I had much to learn about God's priorities in life. The apostle Paul wrote that the quality of a man's relationship at home is a major factor in his qualification for Christian ministry.

A major crisis came in January 1967 when I was in Switzerland, without Anne and Fiona, speaking at the winter sports party organised by the Officers' Christian Union. In many ways it was a wonderful time when we saw God powerfully at work in people's lives; but the asthma became increasingly severe, possibly aggravated by the high altitude, and after two or three hopeless nights of total sleeplessness, a decision was made to fly me home a few days before the party was over. When I saw Anne at the railway station, I noticed her look of anxiety, gave her a weak smile but scarcely had the breath to say 'Hallo'. Anne had to push me along the platform as I sat, wheezing and coughing, on a porter's trolley.

Like a madman, as I see it now, I was off the next month to lead another university mission, this time in Trinity College, Dublin; but once again had to leave two days early due to severe asthma. By this time something had to be done. Reluctantly I cancelled another university mission, in Durham, which I had been booked to lead ten days later, as my condition was becoming serious.

Once I was so ill that Anne sent for our doctor in the early hours of the morning. I had been struggling for breath, and was so disorientated through lack of oxygen that I apparently asked Anne, at 3 a.m., if she was my optician! What I thought I was doing in bed with my optician at three in the morning I cannot begin to imagine! Our doctor duly arrived and gave me an injection, but it had no effect whatsoever. I was still gasping for breath. He gave me another injection which eased the situation a little, and he came back first thing in the morning with a consultant to ask for his professional advice. The consultant explained that normally he would send me to hospital straight away, but since Anne was a nurse he was prepared to take the risk of sending the two of us, plus Fiona of course, away from York for three months' convalescence.

As I think about it now, I suppose it was a partial breakdown. Although it was a relief to be away from all responsibilities for a time – I could not think straight about anything – I felt utterly crushed by the apparent implications of it all. The work in York was beginning to be really exciting. St. Cuthbert's Church had been packed out for several Sundays, and we were having to apply for an extension to seating in the church. The Thursday Fellowship had also grown fast, and we were now relaying the Bible study to several rooms in the rectory because so many people wanted to come. The universities, too, had unexpectedly opened up, and God was apparently using me for effective evangelism among students. My first book, on youth work, called *Towards Tomorrow's Church*, had been published and was well received. Everything seemed on the point of blossoming.

As I went away from it all for those three months, depression initially set in. I genuinely thought I would never preach again, never return to the work in York, never lead another mission, never write another book, and never really cope as a husband and father. I felt a complete and total failure in virtually every area of my life. I had come to an end of myself. My natural strength had failed, and I had to release to the Lord all that had become very dear in my heart. It may be that I had come to love the Lord's work more than the Lord himself. Whatever were the spiritual reasons for that painful period, I had to hand back everything I knew to the Lord, and humbly, with empty hands, ask for his mercy, healing and grace. The future was totally uncertain, and all I could hope for was the Lord himself. The one thing I could do during those three months was to spend the time with Anne and Fiona. And that was the best thing possible.

9

St. Cuthbert's – Growth

'Your absence has been such a blessing to us!' was the greeting we received on our return to York. It was good to know that we were not indispensable, and we took that delightfully ambiguous remark as a sign that God had by now established his work in York, at least at a foundational level. Others had taken on the responsibilities and had grown spiritually as a result.

The three months away from York had also been of considerable blessing to us as a family. In spite of all the traumas and tensions Anne and I had known, we still loved each other very much – which is probably why the tensions had been so traumatic. The time we had together, doing nothing except enjoying each other's company and taking constant delight in Fiona, reinforced our love, and in the peacefulness of those weeks my asthma subsided. By the end of our convalescence I was able to think about the work without always provoking another spasm, and I realised, after this period of humbling and chastening, that my work for the Lord had not yet come to an end. In York, in fact, things had only just started.

During 1966 I had preached often about the Person and work of the Holy Spirit, and spoke simply about the spiritual renewal that God was now bringing all over the world. From that time onwards, a growing number within our congregation were not only finding a personal relationship with Christ, but were also consciously being filled with the Spirit. Some were speaking in tongues, mostly in private in their own personal prayer life, but occasionally in public during prayer meetings, providing an 'interpretation' followed.

Some were also beginning to prophesy as they shared what they felt God was saying to us, and we saw immediately how immensely edifying this gift could be in the life of a congregation. It was never a substitute for the regular teaching from the Scriptures, but God could use a simple message to touch the hearts of his people in a remarkably personal way. We could see why the apostle Paul wrote so positively about this gift in 1 Corinthians 14.

We discovered the value of prophecy in evangelism too. A student came to our church one evening, brought by her Christian friend. The student was not a Christian herself, and she was embarrassed to discover that it was a Communion service. Feeling increasingly out of place within that atmosphere of joyful corporate worship, she walked out of the service half-way through. Later, however, she realised that she had left her scarf behind, so she returned when she thought that the service would be over. Since we had come to the end of the administration of the bread and the wine, the girl went up to the front pew to collect her scarf. At that moment there was silence, following a flow of continuous praise, and then two members of the congregation brought words of prophecy that they thought they had received from God. The student wrote to me the next day: 'I heard my actual thoughts in the second prophecy – something I have never heard before. I heard God actually telling me, in a church with hundreds of other people present, not to run as I had done so often before . . . I felt and experienced God's presence – something terrifying yet wonderful.' There and then she surrendered her life to Christ. The apostle Paul once wrote: 'If all prophesy, and an unbeliever or outsider enters, . . . the secrets of his heart are disclosed; and so, falling on his face, he will worship God and declare that God is really among you' (1 Cor. 14:24f). This is exactly what happened with the girl. We had hundreds of instances when God spoke directly to both Christians and non-Christians alike, all with

positive results affecting people's lives and drawing them
closer to Christ.

We also prayed much for gifts of healing: some were
healed, and some were not. The whole ministry of healing left
us often puzzled and confused, having to bow before the
sovereign purposes of God; and yet when prayer for healing
was sensitively handled, there was always a blessing in one
form or another. We discovered also the values of the gifts of
'knowledge' and 'wisdom'. Sometimes God gave us by his
Spirit an insight into the real and hidden needs of a person
who obviously needed God's help, and we were able to get to
the heart of the problem quite quickly. During all the years
that followed there was never once a split in the congregation
over this issue of spiritual gifts.

Many other gifts were developing, too. I was particularly
encouraged to see spontaneous gifts of evangelism emerging.
People who had found the reality of God in their lives talked
naturally to their friends about Christ. Some were brought to
the regular 'Guest Services' which we held about six times a
year, when we would try to explain, as simply as we could,
how anyone could find Christ. Many did. At the first service,
only one young schoolgirl responded. She courageously
pushed her way through the stream of the congregation as
they were leaving the church. She was Pauline Hornby, a
York girl, who became a faithful and much-loved member of
our congregation for years, later joining my full-time travelling team for four years, before marrying our assistant organist, Andrew Shepherd. At each subsequent Guest Service we
saw any number, from three at the least to eighty at the most,
outwardly profess faith in Christ, although there were doubtless many more we did not know about at the time. Consequently these Guest Services became well known and
popular, and soon they had to be relayed to a nearby hall
because St. Cuthbert's, now packed to the doors, could hold
no more. Later, a regular closed-circuit television system had
to be installed for all the evening services, as the numbers
steadily increased. The Family Services, too, had a 'repeat
performance' each Sunday morning.

With good New Testament precedent, we had numerous house meetings also. We were aware that a new Christian has many friends, neighbours and colleagues who are not true believers, so that he is in an ideal situation for sharing his faith with them. We found, too, that these friends were interested in hearing more about all this, and were quite willing to come into the informal atmosphere of a home where a speaker would give a short talk, followed often by a lively discussion. It was a marvellous and natural sphere for evangelism, and at most of the many house meetings that were held for this purpose we saw at least one person become a Christian as a result. We felt much the same as St. Luke when he wrote about Samaria 2,000 years ago, 'There was much joy in that city.' It was a time of spontaneous and joyful expansion.

The vision of our church as a resource centre for students was also being fulfilled. Large numbers of students came to us from York University, St. John's College of Education, and other colleges nearby; and over the years a great many students came to Christ as a result, or were strengthened in their faith. We also had a simple hospitality scheme, linking students with families in our congregation wherever possible. Many deep friendships were formed in this way, and students loved getting away from campus life every now and then to spend time, often a Sunday, in ordinary family life. As the work grew we were often able to make one or more of our full-time staff available for counselling students, and naturally we worked closely whenever we could with the chaplains concerned.

In this way we saw ourselves in a serving, supportive role. We did not mean to offer a substitute for Christian fellowship and witness on the campus itself (if students are not committed to the evangelism of students, however tough that might be at times, no one else will be), but it seemed obvious that one or more churches in the city could help student Christians to feel a part of the wider church. Indeed, we specifically sought to help students prepare for the transition from their rather specialised activities at college or university to membership of local churches after they left. It was also possible,

through our ordinary Sunday services, to give students a taste
of worship and of the body of Christ which they could never
have known in the enclosed community on the campus itself.
Many of them were also able to benefit from the regular
preaching they heard, and significantly there were comparatively few tensions in York University, for example, over
some 'charismatic' issues compared with some problems in
other universities. Today it is a constant joy meeting active
Christians in many walks of life – not a few on the mission field
or in the ordained ministry – who first became Christians
during their student days in York, partly at least as a result of
what they had experienced at our church.

The heart of the congregation was also growing in depth
and maturity, although we were still a very young church. The
number at the Parish Fellowship each Thursday was regularly
about 140, filling six rooms to capacity in the rectory. The
Bible study was relayed to the rooms and followed by a time
of prayer within each room. As every mid-week meeting in
the church had to take place in the rectory (there was nowhere
else available), it was not easy for Anne, especially when
Fiona was woken by the constant coming and going, with bells
ringing and doors slamming; but somehow we managed it –
often at the cost of depression for Anne, asthma for me, and
tensions between us.

It would obviously be wrong for me to suggest that, during
those early years, we knew nothing but pain and tears. Our
love for one another was always there, in spite of many stormy
scenes, and we had some hilarious moments as well. With so
many people coming to the rectory each week, we found it
difficult having only one lavatory, and that was up a flight of
stairs. A friend of mine, who was an officer in the army
stationed at Catterick, said that his soldiers were doing
nothing much, and so volunteered a work-party to build us
another lavatory in a downstairs passage. After considerable
difficulty they found the necessary plans showing the position
of the water pipes and drains, and the council's permission
was obtained. The soldiers then dug, through thick clay soil, a
huge trench which wound its way gradually round our home.

By now winter had set in, and with the back door frequently left open as soldiers went to and fro for cups of tea and visits to the one lavatory, the rectory became an ice-box. When the trench was at its largest, all the troops were suddenly posted overseas, and we were left with an impressive moat round our house, which rapidly filled with water and ice. One night an unfortunate tramp actually fell in, becoming covered with wet clay which he then brought into the house. With all the pressures of work, asthma and general inefficiency, I am afraid it was months before I filled the trench in. Few tramps visited us after that, and we waited for almost ten years before our second 'loo' was installed.

My outside speaking engagements were now increasing rapidly, especially in universities; and during the ensuing years I led missions at Cambridge, Oxford, Durham, Southampton, Keele, Sussex, Manchester, Birmingham, Aston, Bangor, Bristol, Leicester, Liverpool, Nottingham, Sheffield, and at various other places, including several universities overseas. Most of these missions proved extraordinarily fruitful, with many hundreds of students finding Christ as a result. Letters kept pouring in. 'I have never known such utter joy and quietness of mind,' said one research student. 'It is like living in a world which suddenly has an extra dimension.' Another wrote, 'I shall never be able to express my gratitude to Christ for the way in which he has become so real and living.' Today it is a constant joy meeting some of those who professed conversion years ago and who are now actively serving Christ in different parts of the world.

Such frequent travelling, however, was an undoubted trial for Anne. Although she knew that it was God's will, which she accepted, each time I went away she experienced a deep sense of rejection and abandonment. This produced tension between us, often for two or three days prior to my departure, so much so that I would often cry in desperation to God on my way to some university, 'O Lord, I'm not sure how much more either Anne or I can take. If you really want me to do this work you will have to give us more grace.'

For Anne, especially, it was a lonely time. With me leading

all the church services and meetings, and often away on other engagements, she was left alone in the rectory with Fiona, missing the fellowship that others were enjoying. I too became anxious because, mainly due to the domestic upheaval which follows the birth of any child, Anne was no longer reading her Bible and praying as she used to – at least not in the regular, disciplined way which had been her pattern in the past, and which was still very much my own. Nevertheless, it was during this period of considerable loneliness and pain that Anne learnt to listen to the Lord, to hear him speak to her. She discovered how to meditate on a word, a phrase, a verse or an aspect of God's character. She found a new way of communicating with the Lord which was not dependent on the regular 'quiet time' of her evangelical heritage. At times she would read her Bible for hours, but at others the Bible was closed for days or even weeks. It was during this period, however, that she began to develop the prophetic ministry that God has especially used to touch the lives of so many people. The irritating thing for me was that despite Anne's haphazard devotional life and my dogged discipline, Anne often seemed much more in touch with Christ than I was! Reluctantly I had to admit (and later to rejoice) that most of the best developments in York over the years came through Anne's prophetic vision, which I had then to work out in my own terms, giving the congregation the necessary biblical teaching for each fresh idea and then leading them in that direction. Invariably, though, it was a direction that Anne had already seen several months, if not years before.

The birth of our second child, Guy, happened in April 1969 in unusual circumstances. We probably got our dates wrong, but according to my diary the child should have been born by about April 8th. Therefore I readily accepted the invitation from a good friend of mine, Dick Lucas, to preach at three of his Tuesday lunch-hour services, on April 15th, 22nd, and 29th. By then Anne and the new baby should have been safely back at home. I was particularly keen to visit again St. Helen's Church in Bishopsgate, London, where Dick Lucas was rector, because of the amazing work among city businessmen that God had developed through him. Although I have now visited a good many cities in many parts of the world I have never seen any comparable work amongst businessmen which has been so thorough and effective. It is truly a remarkable demonstration of the power of God through the straight-forward proclamation of his word in the Bible.

I became increasingly apprehensive, however, as April 15th and 22nd came and went, and still no baby had been born. Early in the morning of the 29th it all started to happen. I rang for the midwife, and then dashed for the station to catch the London train since I had to preach my third sermon at St. Helen's that lunch-hour (my priorities still needed a drastic overhaul!). When I arrived at St. Helen's I rang the Maternity Hospital. 'Put the phone down at once,' snapped the nurse at the other end. 'It's all happening right now!' Five minutes before the service was due to start I nervously rang again. 'You have a son, and both are doing fine!' The subject of that sermon had been advertised some weeks before: it was 'The New Birth'! Nonchalantly I said from the pulpit, almost as an aside, 'Ten minutes ago a son was born to me in York.' I was told that the few women present (the church is always packed out with men) ceased to listen to another word, their minds captivated by the thought of that new-born baby. But I could not resist the evangelistic challenge that this provided. 'My wife was three weeks overdue,' I said, not entirely sure of my medical knowledge. 'Had it gone on much longer, it would have been dangerous for her. Some of you, spiritually speaking, are not three weeks overdue. You are thirty to forty years overdue. If you go on much longer it may be dangerous for you. Jesus said that you *must* be born again.' The effect was quite dramatic.

We were obviously overjoyed with Guy's birth and praised God for the gift of a son as well as a daughter. But once again we experienced broken nights for at least nine months, with few exceptions, leading to more exhaustion, more asthma, more tension and further 'interruptions' to the work. Yet through it all God was continuing to bless the church in York and the missions in the universities.

There is always a mysterious and inescapable link between suffering and blessing. The apostle Paul knew much about this, and he learnt to be 'content with weaknesses, insults, hardships, persecutions and calamities; for' he said, 'when I am weak, then am I strong'. It was when he was weak that the power of Christ especially rested upon him (2 Cor. 12:7-10). Indeed he realised that God had actually given him 'a thorn in the flesh'. No one knows what this was, but most commentators believe that it was some physical handicap. God used it to keep him weak enough to receive grace for usefulness. He was promised sufficient grace, 'for my strength is made perfect in weakness'. I came to view my asthma as a 'thorn in the flesh'. Like Paul, I asked for it to be removed; but constantly I have found that God's grace is sufficient in all my weakness, and his presence has always been evident in any suffering we have known. Human weakness makes room for divine grace. Our story is not one of human achievement, human wisdom, or human greatness, and our church in York bears testimony to divine grace given during a continuing experience of weakness, physical and spiritual, out of which came the joy of new life.

It is sometimes said that whereas God loves us just as we are, he loves us too much to leave us as we are. J. B. Phillips once wrote a book called *Your God Is Too Small*. It is a good title, since most of us have a much too narrow vision of God. I soon discovered that God was now wanting to expand my own vision of him in ways that brought me a 'sunshine of surprises'.

10

Widening Vision

A significant milestone in my life came through an international conference for spiritual renewal organised by the Fountain Trust at Guildford in 1971. Michael and Jeanne Harper had courageously sought to encourage renewal within the Church, in spite of considerable misunderstanding and opposition, and Anne and I had already benefited from a number of Fountain Trust conferences they had promoted, as we tried to gain a clearer grasp of what God was doing by his Spirit. The conference at Guildford, based at Surrey University, proved particularly challenging as it was the first time that I found myself, as a speaker, on the same platform as Roman Catholic speakers. Since my conversion, I had come to think that the Roman Catholic Church was an apostate Church: it effectively denied the great Reformation doctrine of 'justification by faith' through its insistence on many religious observances as necessary to salvation; it exalted the Virgin Mary to a position that seemed at times even greater than that of Christ himself; it taught that the bread and wine at the Mass became mystically the body and blood of Christ; it gave Papal infallibility and Roman Catholic dogma an authority equal to that of the New Testament; it undermined the truths of salvation by its teaching about purgatory and by its prayers for the dead. In other words, it preached 'another gospel'; and the apostle Paul once wrote that anyone doing such a thing would be cursed by God! For me, the Roman Catholic Church was virtually synonymous with the anti-Christ: a massive and powerful organisation that had all the form of the Christian religion but was in fact a Satanic conterfeit of the real thing. My 'anti-Rome' attitude was almost akin to that of the most extreme Protestants in Northern Ireland, although I was less vocal about it. Nevertheless I was totally convinced of the truth of my own convictions, although I confess that very rarely did I actually talk to Roman Catholics, and still less did I attempt to listen to what they were saying.

Once or twice in Cambridge I discussed the matter with Dr. Basil Atkinson, whose own attitude towards Catholics was even more colourful than my own. There was always a delightful eccentricity about Basil which could shock those who did not know him at all; but anyone who knew him realised how much he loved the Lord and how much he loved all those who knew Jesus personally, as he manifestly did. Therefore, in spite of his strongly anti-Roman background, I remember Basil once asking me if I thought it were possible for Roman Catholic nuns to be saved. 'Why do you ask?' I replied. 'Because I have just met two nuns who seemed to be radiant for Jesus. It seemed impossible, and yet it was true!' After that day I too met quite a number of Catholic nuns, priests and laity who also gave me the same impression, and I had to do some theological gymnastics to cope with it. However, these were still my own private thoughts, and I had not yet made any public comment about them.

The conference at Guildford was quite another matter. How could I share the same platform with leaders from an apostate Church? And, by so doing, was I not compromising the truths for which many of the Reformers had died? I took the risk, and cautiously engaged in conversation with some of the Catholics present who were theologically articulate. Two facts came home to me. First, they showed me much more love and acceptance than I was able to show them. Second, when we got down to the basic issues – justification by faith, the finished work of Christ on the cross, the place of the Virgin Mary, the doctrine of the Mass, and supreme authority of Scripture – I was quite astonished to find that some of the problems had been purely a question of 'semantics' (using words in different ways). The more I listened the more I was impressed by the biblical position that they held. We did not agree totally about everything; but concerning many essential elements of the Gospel there seemed little if any difference. I also realised that some of this had been directly the result of the renewing work of the Spirit in their own minds and hearts (the Holy Spirit is always the Spirit of truth), and I felt that some of the views of those present at this conference were not typical of official Catholic teaching, at least not before Vatican II (1963–5). How then could they remain in the Roman Catholic Church and not demonstrate their new life in Christ by coming out of it?

As I thought and prayed about this, I felt that God was saying something to me: 'David, I'm not first and foremost concerned about your convictions, but I am concerned about your attitudes. And your attitudes towards those with whom you do not agree are all wrong. First get your attitudes right, and then we can talk about your convictions.' I wanted to protest, because on various important issues I was so sure that I was right and that others (not only Roman Catholics) were wrong. But Paul once wrote, 'And if . . . I understand . . . all knowledge . . . but have not love, I am nothing.' Those words hit me very powerfully. I began to repent deeply of my negative, critical attitudes. I confessed my spiritual arrogance. I acknowledged my lack of love towards others, especially towards professing Christians with whom I did not agree. The battle was not won overnight – far from it, in fact. But as I continued to ask the Spirit of God to change my negative attitudes I found that God was giving me an altogether new love towards many non-evangelicals, even Roman Catholics.

What is more, as my attitudes changed, so I began to listen to people – some of them for the first time. I began to hear what they really believed, not what I thought they believed. I discovered vast numbers of true brothers and sisters in Christ whom I never knew existed. I tried to believe the best about people instead of always fearing the worst. I learnt that God had many things to teach me, often through those from

different traditions than my own. I began to see how rich and
varied is the world-wide Body of Christ, and I praised God for
releasing me from the spiritual blinkers that I had worn for so
long. The sovereignty of God, working in different ways
amongst different people, was more wonderful than I had
ever previously understood. Even passages of Scripture
spoke to me in new ways as I tried to fathom a little more the
'depth of the riches and wisdom and knowledge of God'.

All these new impressions were confirmed many times over
in the ensuing years, and often I had remarkable times of
fellowship with all sorts of people I would never have associated with previously. One unforgettable experience was the
Third National Conference on Charismatic Renewal in Ireland, at the Royal Dublin Society Showground, in September
1976. I had gone as the opening speaker, and was amazed to
find 6,000 present, of whom 5,000 were Roman Catholic
including many hundreds of nuns and priests, and the rest
were Protestants of all denominations. It was an incredible
conference. I was especially impressed by the God-centred,
Christ-centred nature of it all. Every meeting began with a
prolonged time of worship; it seemed that the people were not
willing to listen to any speaker until they had first fixed their
minds and hearts on God himself. It was the Lord whom they
wanted to hear, not just some ordinary speaker! Equally
obvious was their hunger for God's word: they loved to hear
the Scriptures expounded. They were also profoundly aware
of the difference between religion and the 'real thing'. It was
astonishing for me to hear Roman Catholic priests from the
platform saying to this vast crowd: 'It is not enough being
born as a Catholic; you need to be born again by the Spirit of
God. It is not enough to come to Mass each week; you need to
know Jesus Christ as your personal Lord and Saviour.' It was
almost like a Billy Graham evangelistic crusade!

Most moving of all was the Service of Reconciliation on the
Saturday night. Led by a small group of Protestant and
Catholic leaders, we saw, from a good exposition of Ephesians 2, that the cause of our divisions in home, Church and
society is always sin in the heart of man. Through simple

drama enacted in front of a huge empty cross, we saw that the only place for reconciliation is at the foot of the cross. When we come to the cross, we come not as Protestants or Roman Catholics, but as sinners; and when we put our trust in the one Saviour who died for our sins once for all, God accepts each one of us as 'My son, my daughter', and this means that we should now say to one another, 'My brother, my sister'. We were then all invited to go to anyone within that huge hall, to ask for forgiveness for anything we had said or done in the past that grieved the Spirit of God. I was at once surrounded by a large crowd of nuns and priests asking for forgiveness from me, as a representative Protestant, for things that they had said and done that were not right; and of course I reciprocated. Then we embraced one another as brothers and sisters, experiencing at a deeper level than I had ever known before what it means to be 'one body through the cross'. If we belonged to Christ, we belonged also to one another; and what God has joined together through the death of his own Son, let not man put asunder.

The next day, in obedience to our respective traditions, we separated for the Catholic Mass and the Protestant Eucharist. Most of us were in tears for much of the service because we felt deep within our hearts (I had never experienced this before) the grief that Christ must feel over his torn, lacerated and divided body here on earth. There are over 20,000 registered Christian denominations alone, quite apart from the tensions and divisions within any given denomination or local church. Ever since that conference I have sensed a little of the pain that Christ must always feel when we separate from one another, when in effect we say to him, 'You died to make us one, and we don't care!' Jesus surely weeps for the state of his Body, the Church, on earth today.

I began to speak more openly about the importance of our oneness in Christ, and the urgent need for reconciliation in the Church if we were to have any credible ministry of reconciliation in the world. At the Nottingham Evangelical Anglican Conference (NEAC) in 1977 I gave one of the Bible Readings, speaking on the Mission of the Church from Luke

10. One of my points was the vital importance of unity, and *in that context* I went on to say that 'in many ways the Reformation was one of the greatest tragedies that ever happened to the Church. Martin Luther,' I explained, 'never wanted to split the Church, simply to reform it. We no doubt glory in the biblical truths that were rediscovered at the Reformation (as I certainly do), but from the Reformation onwards the Body of Christ in the world has been torn from limb to limb into hundreds of separate pieces.' When I called the Reformation one of the 'greatest tragedies' in the Church, there was an audible gasp in the conference hall. In the context in which it was said, it was a perfectly fair statement. If only the Church of 1517 had been willing for the reformation that Martin Luther, himself a Roman Catholic monk, had tried to effect, we might never have divided into these thousands of little fragments.

That sentence was inevitably a gift-horse for any journalist: 'David Watson says that the Reformation was the greatest tragedy in the history of the Church!' Taken out of its context it sounded worse than heresy to any warm-blooded Protestant. I had many stinging and condemning letters sent to me from some of my Reformed brethren, and I still receive the occasional one. Some will never forgive me for that remark, and would like to see it inscribed on my tombstone, no doubt! Yet, having repented of my own critical attitudes (and I keep on having to do so), I longed that a new spirit of repentance should come upon the Church. I could see this as an absolute priority before any revival came: 'If my people who are called by my name humble themselves, and pray and seek my face, and turn from their wicked ways, then I will hear from heaven, and will forgive their sin and heal their land' (2 Chron. 7:14). For example, with all the division in Northern Ireland which has perpetuated the violence there for so many years, there can surely be no true healing of relationships until there is first a deep repentance – not just for the sin of violence, but even more for the sin of bitterness which lies at the heart of the troubles there.

The same principle is true wherever we Christians do not

love one another as Christ has loved us, nor welcome one another as Christ has welcomed us, nor forgive one another as Christ has forgiven us. Until we sort out our relationships with one another, our relationship with God is not right; and he waits for us to repent before he can renew us with his Spirit of love and truth.

When I was leading a festival of praise in St. Anne's Cathedral, Belfast, both Protestants and Roman Catholics were warmly invited, and a number of priests and nuns were present. Some rather militant Protestants picketed the service outside the main doors, and handed out tracts to everyone coming in. One of these tracts showed a lot of ants marching towards Rome. They apparently represented us, since we were Protest-ants who had left out the protest in what we were doing. We were therefore only 'ants' heading stupidly in a Popish direction. It was a rather sick joke, except that it was meant to be deadly serious. How much is the spirit of repentance needed among us all!

A further development in my vision of God and his work came in the summer of 1972 when Anne and I left Fiona and Guy with Anne's parents in Cheshire and went for several weeks to North America, on an exchange-of-preaching scheme organised by the British Council of Churches. Among many fascinating experiences, we were particularly struck by the quality of worship that we experienced in an Episcopal church in Virginia. In many respects there was nothing much to write home about: the musicians and singers were not unusually talented. But they had about them a gentle quality of intimate worship which was like a cup of cold water to someone in the desert. It was enormously refreshing. They were obviously singing not just *about* the Lord, but *to* the Lord, and their worship brought a sense of God's presence into the service in a quiet but most effective way.

That was followed shortly afterwards by a morning service at St. Margaret's Community Centre in Vancouver, where the pastor was Bob Birch. Bob was one of those men whom you might not look at twice in the street; there was nothing outwardly impressive about him. But his whole life was totally

directed towards Christ, and he was one of the most prayerful
and godly men I had ever met. However, what struck us much
more than the pastor was the church itself. We had never been
anywhere before where we had felt so completely overwhelmed by love. As I looked around that packed church –
people were sitting everywhere – I noticed an amazing mixture of ages and backgrounds. All the normal social and
cultural barriers were broken down by the love of Christ.
Barefoot students in jeans were sitting next to bank managers
in pin-stripe suits. And the worship was simply glorious.
Everyone seemed totally absorbed in the act of loving Christ
through praise and prayer. You could see from their faces that
almost all those present were profoundly aware of his living
presence in our midst, and once again they were singing *to* the
Lord. The service, although non-liturgical, was ordered and
dignified; yet at the same time there was a spontaneity and
freedom about it so that words of prophecy and singing in
tongues seemed perfectly natural and in no way contrived.

The whole hour was broadcast every Sunday through local
radio, and calls were coming in all the time from people in
need in different parts of Vancouver. Without any fuss, teams
would go out immediately to those calls for help, so that the
service had an immediacy and relevance about it that was
unmistakable. I preached for about twenty minutes and, after
another hymn, the service over the radio came to an end. But
the congregation in the church went on for another hour or so,
with more free worship, praise, prayer and the exercise of
spiritual gifts – all of which proved intensely edifying – and
then I discovered that I was expected to preach again! Quickly
I put a few thoughts together from Ephesians 5, and preached
rather clumsily my second sermon. Several people nevertheless came forward for counselling. Then, after the final hymn
and benediction, a woman sang exquisitely in a 'tongue', both
language and music given by the Holy Spirit, and then sang,
equally exquisitely, the interpretation of the tongue. What I
found especially moving and humbling was that, in that short
sung word in the Spirit, that woman had perfectly summed up
what I had been struggling to say in my second twenty-minute

sermon! I learnt later that the woman had normally quite an unimpressive voice; but when it was controlled by the Spirit it certainly had a breath of heaven about it. As Anne and I left that church we felt that if God was anywhere on the face of this earth, he surely was in that service that morning.

Through those fleeting experiences in Virginia and Vancouver, God increased my vision to an altogether new understanding of worship, and gave me a fresh glimpse of the body of Christ in action. Up to that point, I was beginning to think that we had now 'arrived' at St. Cuthbert's, because the work had been developing so rapidly. Now I knew that we had so much more to learn, and I was thrilled with the prospects of new horizons opening up. An official report on our church commented: 'Members of the congregation noticed a much more liberated minister when he returned to St. Cuthbert's, and there was greater freedom, joy and spontaneity in worship . . . Praise became the dominant note.' It was not that we had lessened our biblical teaching – far from it. However we were giving a lot of positive teaching about the primacy and nature of worship. I had seen, almost as if it were for the first time, the rich variety of worship mentioned in the psalms. I realised, too, how straitjacketed we had become with our stilted, formal services, or with our hearty evangelical hymns. How little we understood about adoration in worship! How stiff we were in any bodily expression! In the Anglican church we were used to kneeling, as a posture symbolising reverence and humility. But how inhibited we were when it came to clapping, raising hands or dancing. Even as a 'much more liberated minister' I was still quite a long way from all that. At the Guildford conference Michael Harper had tried to encourage us to lift up our hands in praise to the Lord, but inwardly I replied 'Not on your life!' Since I was standing next to the Dean of the Cathedral I told myself that I would not raise my hands anyway, so as not to embarrass him; but I was the one who was irritated by this un-English display of religious fervour. Yet it was a problem which hardly anyone else at the conference seemed to have!

All this fresh stimulus was preparing us for a major step

11

St. Michael-le-Belfrey, York

A letter arrived one morning from a friend asking why on earth the Diocese had not offered me St. Michael-le-Belfrey Church, just opposite York Minster. St. Michael's was almost three times the size of St. Cuthbert's, almost empty and all but redundant. Plans for making it redundant had been completed after two years of hard work, and the documents were just waiting for the Archbishop's signature. Rather like St. Cuthbert's, St. Michael's was also destined to become a museum, this time for the Minster.

Two or three years before, I had tentatively approached various Diocesan officials about the possibility of moving into St. Michael's, but had been given a polite but firm refusal. If the idea was right, the timing was wrong. But now, through the excellent work of the Archdeacon of York, the Venerable Leslie Stanbridge, backed strongly by Morris Maddocks, the Bishop of Selby, and Donald Coggan, the Archbishop of York, a provisional experimental scheme of moving the congregation from St. Cuthbert's to St. Michael's went through within two months – it must have broken all records in the Church of England! On January 1st, 1973 we moved our Sunday services from one building to the other. This was to prove much more significant than we could possibly have imagined at the time.

One month before that, however, there was another unusual development. I had been waiting for a train at York station one day, when a good friend of mine, a member of our congregation, said, 'David, have you ever thought of holding

our Guest Services in York Minster?' To be honest, the idea
had never even crossed my mind. I knew that we were packed
out at both the church and the relay rooms, but St. Cuthbert's
was really a very small building and the Minster was the
biggest Gothic cathedral in the world. Even with our Guest
Service congregation of about 700, we would be lost in the
Minster. Nevertheless, encouraged by this friend, I
approached one or two of the Minster canons to discover their
reactions. The Minster had recently gone through extensive
works, costing about £3 million, when its crumbling foundations were strengthened, a magnificent undercroft opened,
the exterior cleaned and the interior decorated. It was now a
superb sight, probably in a finer state of glory than it had ever
been in its long history. At the Rededication Service of the
Minster, after all the repairs and cleaning had finished, the
Archbishop of York said that he hoped the building would not
just be a monument but the very gate to heaven to thousands
who came within its walls.

The Minster clergy I talked to were surprisingly positive
about my strange enquiry, and they agreed that we could
organise an Advent Guest Service in the Minster on Decem-
ber 3rd. They gave me every possible help in planning this. At
times I was afraid that we had attempted an impossible task,
and that at least half of the huge nave would be quite empty.
However, the media got hold of this extraordinary idea of a
tiny parish church holding its service in the vast Minster, and
there was a fair amount of free and unexpected publicity from
the press, radio and television. The result was that the
Minister was not only full to its seating capacity, but extra
chairs were rapidly brought in, and many were sitting on
kneelers on the floor. It turned out to be a most wonderful
service, and that night many gave their lives to Christ.

The Minster clergy seemed just as delighted as we were;
and thus encouraged by them, we began a series of Minster
services (about six a year), to which coach parties would come
from a wide area. Many clergy and ministers closed down
their evening services in country areas, and brought most of
their congregations with them. It is hard to know quite why

they came, but the services had a popular appeal, both in the themes we took and in the way in which those themes were developed. We taught explicitly from the Bible, trying to relate its message to the obvious issues of the day; and we set the teaching in the context of joyful worship, led not only by the organ but also by a singing group accompanied by a variety of instruments. Later our worship was often interpreted by dance, and my sermons were illustrated by drama. We erected a large stage half-way down one side of the long central nave, and arranged all the chairs around the stage, so that there was much better visual contact with everyone in the congregation. Jesus once described the kingdom of heaven in terms of a sumptuous marriage feast, something enormously attractive to hungry people: 'Come, all is now ready!' The great Jewish festivals had been times of marvellous celebration, marked by colour and music and singing and dancing, as the mighty acts of God were retold. It is in this depressing age of today that the Christian Church learns again how to celebrate, so that we not only talk about the magnificent banquet of the Gospel but let people experience it through the joyful and festive context in which the Gospel is proclaimed. Can this really be conveyed by a procession of clergy at the start of a cathedral service? Often this resembles more the awkward shuffling of grim-faced penguins! Why not recapture some of the colourful drama of those superb Jewish festivals, knowing that their hopes and expectations were now fulfilled in Christ? I can easily understand why the psalmist said, 'I was glad when they said unto me, Let us go to the house of the Lord' – it was such a glorious occasion. As we attempted to set the jewel of Christ in the crown of celebration, we found that many wanted to be there. All those special Minster services were occasions of much mutual encouragement, and many hundreds came to a personal knowledge of Christ. It exceeded all our possible expectations, and also gave us an excellent relationship with the clergy of the Minster, which was most important now that we had become immediate neighbours.

We had begun to see, too, that the timing of our move to St.

Michael-le-Belfrey was just right. Not only was the building saved at the last moment from becoming redundant (which in itself would have been a negative witness to the relevance of the Christian faith for today), but the style and setting of the building was utterly appropriate to the next phase of God's work amongst us. In St. Cuthbert's we were out on a limb, experimenting freely with services, largely doing our own thing (trying hard to be meaningful), but paying only lip-service to the Anglican liturgy. In St. Michael-le-Belfrey, however, we were at the heart of a famous city, next to a famous Minster and under the gracious but eagle eye of a famous Archbishop.

Once the costly job of cleaning, decorating and rewiring the building had been finished, we gradually became aware of the new responsibilities that God had given us. York is a tourist city, attracting each year about two and a half million visitors from all over the world, and all of them, with hardly an exception, came to our very doorstep to look at the Minster. Added to that, the growth of God's work amongst us was beginning to be known throughout Great Britain and further afield, and we found an increasing number of visitors joining us for our Sunday services. When members of our own congregation were away on holiday in August, as many as eighty per cent of the 700 present could be visitors.

We saw the responsibility of all this in two complementary ways. First, if the renewing work of the Spirit is of any significance at all, it must be worked out within the mainline denominations. In Ezekiel's vision of the valley of the dry bones, when the wind of the Spirit came, the bones were not blown away as being dead and useless. God could have done that, and created new people in their place. In fact, however, the bones came together, were clothed with flesh, and God breathed his life into them. I was (and still am) convinced that God's purpose is to renew the dry bones of existing Christian traditions, and we should not try to bypass them in favour of something more immediately exciting. It always saddens me when I see Christians leave their denominations to join a new independent church; it is precisely in this way that all the

20,800 denominations in the world today came into being in
the first place. Jesus weeps over our self-destructive divisions,
which only help to deny the Gospel that we try to preach. In
St. Michael's, therefore, we became more consciously Anglican, even though my work was becoming increasingly
ecumenical. If the renewal of the Spirit had no place in the
Anglican tradition (or in any other mainline tradition), it was
of no value at all. So we adopted the new Anglican liturgies
since these represented the liturgical renewal of various
Christian traditions around the world. We did not want St.
Michael's to have an independent identity all of its own. We
were not out to build our own empire, with our own order of
service different from everyone else. We were a tiny part of
the 'one holy catholic and apostolic Church' and felt it
important to maintain a clear visible identity with that
Church. When the Archbishop came, for example, we did not
have suddenly to change our pattern of service; it was just the
same format as anyone else might find on any Sunday in the
year, with rare exceptions. Only as we came clearly under the
authority of the Church could we be of any service to the
Church. In fact, the more we willingly and gladly submitted
ourselves to those over us in the Lord, the more the blessing
of God seemed to be upon us.

Secondly, together with this important development, we
learned to discover 'freedom within form'. Once we accepted
the form of the Anglican liturgy as our basic identity (everyone has some identifiable form, even the most 'independent'
churches), we found that there is plenty of freedom within
that form. For example, in this latter part of the twentieth
century we should not be tied only to the hymns and music of
the eighteenth and nineteenth centuries. Some of those
hymns are almost timeless, but many songs and hymns are
being written now to express the life of the Spirit in today's
Church. Through the marvellous ministry of the Fisherfolk
we learned the combination of dignity and joy, depth and
simplicity, quality and gentleness, spiritual sensitivity and
artistic skill. Countless people today are hurting, often because of the pain of broken relationships; but through the

gentleness of worship the Spirit of God can touch and heal those inner wounds. When members of our own congregation later began to write and compose songs, we found that the songs that had that special quality of tenderness about them usually were born out of suffering and tears.

It was in St. Michael's, too, that we learned about the more visual expressions of worship and communication of the Gospel. Most traditional church buildings make drama, mime or dance virtually impossible. Narrow chancels, restricting choir pews, massive pulpits or huge pillars eliminate all but the preacher and choir. It was just the same in St. Michael's; but a careful inspection of the choir pews (by me) revealed some woodworm. Admittedly there was not a lot, but enough to cause us to rip them out altogether, leaving a marvellous space between the front pews and the communion rails – a space that we subsequently used to considerable advantage every Sunday. During a visit to Christchurch Cathedral in New Zealand, I was particularly impressed by a simple design for a large stage which enabled the structure to be erected or dismantled within a matter of minutes. The Dean of Christchurch kindly gave me a copy of the design, and we built a similar one ourselves. It was, and is, in constant use as we began to learn about relevant communication for the world of today, still holding firm to the traditions of the Church to which we belonged.

During this time of settling into St. Michael's, the small congregation that had kept the church from closing needed much grace to welcome the hundreds who came from St. Cuthbert's. It was not easy for them. In spite of being true to the basic Anglican liturgy, the style of music, worship and most other things were clearly different. A few of the original congregation stayed, including Peter Gibson, one of the church-wardens and the Minster glazier, a world expert on stained glass. Peter soon won everyone's affection by his wise diplomacy, a humble serving spirit and a great sense of humour. But others found the crowds and changes difficult and found a quieter home in the Minster. This was sad, but quite understandable. Journalists occasionally tried to draw out from me unfavourable comments about the Minster services since their style was obviously much more formal than our own. Always I resisted this. I refused to say – or even think – that we were right and they were wrong. Their style of worship was no doubt just as valid, but it was mostly for more traditional Anglicans. We were attempting to make the same basic traditions live for those with little or no church background, but who had become spiritually alive in Jesus Christ.

Over the years we had seen many individuals and families brought to Christ and filled with the Spirit. My short visit with Anne to North America, however, had given us an altogether new understanding of worship and of the Body of Christ; and I began to be aware that we had much more to learn in both these directions before we could share more widely anything significant about the renewal of the Church.

Of course, it is one thing to have a vision of all this, and quite another to work out how that vision could possibly be implemented. In many churches, some of the desired gifts seem either to be absent or not yet developed; and anyway those who may be gifted in certain ways are usually far too busy to give more than a very limited part of their time to the work and mission of the Church. We had to discover ways of releasing men and women for the work to which God might be calling them.

12

The Growth of Community

'I think we ought to share our home with others,' Anne said to me one day.

'We've done that already,' I replied defensively. 'All sorts of people have stayed in our house for longer or shorter periods. We've hardly been on our own since we moved to York.'

'Yes, but they've only been lodgers, such as those university students, or close friends. There are so many others whose primary problem is loneliness, who need to belong to a family. And anyway, we must learn to share our lives together if we're ever truly going to be the Body of Christ.'

I was slowly discovering that Anne had a visionary and prophetic ministry, although I usually questioned it very carefully. With some hesitation I agreed to open our home, a little at a time, to those who were willing to come not as lodgers, but as part of what soon became a community. Anne's vision was much wider than she initially revealed. She felt that a community of shared lives would deepen the sense of community throughout the whole church, even though the majority of our congregation would not adopt this lifestyle. We had the obvious model of the early church who had 'all things in common', and the strength and credibility of their witness lay largely in the quality of their corporate life together. 'See how these Christians love one another!' was the cry of the pagan observer.

Anne also saw that extended households could considerably facilitate ministries within the Church. The cry of most churches is lack of money and shortage of manpower (or personpower, to be non-sexist!). Most churches cannot get anything like the workers they could use, and, even if they could find the personnel, they could never pay for them. However, by sharing our homes and possessions, we could release both money and people for the work of the kingdom of God.

It was fascinating to see, in the following years, that both these visions which Anne saw so clearly were fulfilled beyond anything that we had imagined possible when we took our first faltering and feeble steps.

To begin with we had little concept of who should join our family. They just came. The first was a girl with a long history of mental instability, who had for many years defeated the care of doctors and psychiatrists. For almost two years she became a marvellous member of our household, opening up our closed lives towards others in need, welcoming everyone with great enthusiasm and cheerfulness, teaching Anne to cater for the large numbers who rapidly filled our house, and dealing swiftly and firmly with those who had just come off drugs but who were secretly trying to pursue the habit. She had at least one girl down to the hospital in no time at all to have her stomach washed out. As much as we loved her, however, we were unable to help her beyond a certain point, partly owing to her natural strength of personality; and very sadly I had to ask her to leave, and return to her own home. I felt a terrible sense of failure, which haunted me for months afterwards, especially when we heard indirectly that she had been going through some rough times. It was an early and painful lesson that not all community living is 'successful', and before long we had to clarify our aims: did God want us to concentrate on those who had special personal problems, or what?

Others came for a whole variety of reasons. Andrew Maries, a gifted musician who later became our Musical Director, originally brought his washing round for Anne to do, at her suggestion, and stayed for a number of meals. He was living a typical bachelor's existence. Before long it was a natural progression that he should join us. For several months I found that he irritated me beyond measure, and no doubt I did the same for him. Temperamentally we seemed such opposites, and everything he said and did drew out the worst in me. I found that community life is not always easy, partly because in the pressure of sharing our lives together we begin to see ourselves as we really are, not as we fondly imagine ourselves to be. Always the Lord is concerned not so much with the situation, however trying or irritating it may be, but with our reaction to that situation. 'Lord,' I said, 'I'm not sure I can stand having Andrew in our house much longer. If you want him to stay here, you must do something about it.' I am not sure what God did about it, or how, but I do know that Andrew stayed in our household for seven years and soon became one of our closest friends. We felt almost bereaved when he moved out to marry Alicia, although of course in another sense we were thrilled to see the two of them come together. Alicia had been a member of our household for three years, before moving out to become a District Midwife, and we had all been extremely fond of her.

Another aim of the extended household was so to develop the reality of brotherhood in the Church that single people should not have to spend much of their time wishing and waiting to get married. In today's society there is such a pressure on a single person to be married, or at least to enter into a sexual relationship with someone, that the disappointments and scars of broken relationships are to be seen everywhere. Jesus, however, called men and women into a new society where they could be first and foremost brothers and sisters in the family of God. Marriage is certainly a gift of God, and to be held in honour by all; but Christ wants us to enjoy a depth of relationship with one another that is not always leading towards a sexual union. Many who enjoy community life find depths of commitment with other people that can release them from the trap of thinking only in terms of marriage or sex. However, within those deeply committed relationships of love and service, we are always delighted when two people eventually get married, especially when they have worked through some of the pressures and problems of a single life in today's permissive society.

It was also a joy to see the rapid growth into maturity that Andrew found during his time with us. As Musical Director he now shows a quality and sensitivity which might not have been there apart from all the blessings and traumas of community life. Through his musical leadership many discover in St. Michael's a gentleness in worship, speaking of joy through pain, that they do not easily find in other places. I can see that just as God rubbed off some of my rough edges through my early abrasive encounters with Andrew (and others!), so God may have used both the riches and tensions of living in an extended household to increase his work of grace in Andrew, whom he was preparing as a worship leader to encourage many churches throughout this country.

Others joined our household for shorter or longer periods of time – the shortest was three months, I think – and our roomy Victorian rectory usually had ten or twelve people living in it, our nuclear family being just four. One girl had only recently left the drug scene, and she had to go before too long, as she needed more specialised care than we could give her. However, our children were especially fond of her during her short stay, and it was with immense sadness that we learnt several years later that she had committed suicide. We had to learn humbly that we could not do everything, and that our ministry within the household had definite limitations. We also had to be willing for people to be with us only for a time – perhaps for quite a short time – and then to let people go peacefully out of our household to some other place. This we found quite difficult, and sadly when one or two people left, our relationships with them afterwards were strained, or even non-existent. This was not right, and we had to learn both how to welcome people and how to release people. Several communities find this difficult. Anyway, for many years there was a lot of coming and going, and beds and other furniture were constantly being moved from one room to another.

'Will you go and see a girl called Teresa?' asked a Roman Catholic sister, who had become a dear friend of ours. 'Teresa comes from an impossible home situation, has absolutely no faith, and has just attempted suicide. She is in a mental hospital, and yet she is a bright sixteen-year-old with quite a future. She simply needs a family.' I went to the hospital with another household member to see Teresa, and it was clear to us immediately that she needed to get out of that hospital as soon as possible and find a home. We took her home with us. Her whole life needed sorting out, but most of all she needed to be loved. Within the growing sense of God's family in our house, Terri soon gave her life to Christ, went back to the Roman Catholic Convent in York to continue her studies, and became a delightful member of our household. Naturally Terri had her difficulties; but it brought us immense joy to see her successful in her exams, going to Stirling University, getting married from our house (we were effectively her family), having a child, and more recently settling in South America as a healthy wife and mother, with a strong Christian commitment. Anne had virtually become Terri's adopted mother – and sister in Christ – and we maintain strong links with her to this day. This was one of many encouragements when we saw the healing power of God's love coming through a community of his people.

For the first two years, this new way of living seemed to threaten many in our church, and we felt distinct opposition. It may have been partly because our relationships within the household became unusually deep, as we related to one another as brothers and sisters in Christ, and possibly others in the church were jealous of the special relationship that some had with 'the rector and his wife'. But I suspect that the opening of our home in this way was an inevitable challenge to those who naturally valued the privacy of their own family life. We had taken great care not to press this way of living on to others, but had taught that it was *one* valid way of expressing Christian community – not the only, and not necessarily the best. I fully understood the sense of threat that many felt, however much we tried to avoid putting pressure on other families to follow suit. I found the exercise extremely difficult myself. 'An Englishman's home is his castle' is the old saying, and I was startled to find out how deep this cultural trait went. To begin with I resented others treating my furniture, my possessions, my money, my car, and sometimes even my clothes, as if they were their own. After our first four months, when I was still very unsure whether or not we were doing the right thing, I went to New Zealand for eight weeks, and at the end of that time I was naturally longing to see again Anne, Fiona and Guy – but not so keen on having to see the rest of the household (three or four others at that stage). On my return, I found a practical joke waiting for me. Knowing that I was every inch a typical Englishman who valued his privacy, they put up three camp beds in my study, and strewed with deliberate untidyness, pyjamas and clothes all over my little sanctuary! I was not amused! Indeed after a journey of some thirty-six hours I was exhausted and disorientated, and the little joke threw me into depression for a few days. Fortunately Betty Pulkingham and the Fisherfolk came to stay with us the day after I returned (with people sleeping everywhere in our house – except in my study), and Betty, with her wisdom and experience, told the household in no uncertain terms that they should never do that again when I returned home from a tour. Apparently a group had done something similar to Graham Pulkingham, then rector of the Church of the Redeemer, Houston, Texas, shortly after they had adopted this community style of living, with equally unfortunate results. We all had much to learn.

We soon found that some clear structure was essential to keep everyone from just 'doing his own thing'. We knew that prayer must be the basis of our household, and almost the only time we could meet regularly together was at 7 a.m., when we would spend about thirty minutes sharing together from the Scriptures and praying for one another and for the needs of that day. It was not always easy to maintain this discipline, but we all recognised the importance of it, so kept each other to this commitment. Usually one of the household would make notes of each person's sharing, and then summarise what it seemed that God was saying to us that day. We often found this helpful, and, as a by-product, it encouraged

all of us to read our Bibles on our own in order to have
something fresh to share each morning. We also had lists of
household duties, with everyone on washing-up rotas, etc.
Each person had also an individual assignment: mine was the
simple task of carrying out the dustbins!

Although Anne and I exercised joint headship over the
household, and to that extent were 'house parents', we
worked hard on developing the brother–sister relationship, so
that everyone had the freedom to 'speak the truth in love'. I
sometimes found it difficult and humbling being rebuked by
someone half my age; but the rebuke was usually justified,
and I learnt to take as well as give. Once a week to begin with
(less often later on) we had a household meeting in the
evening, when we would share together at greater length,
raise anything on our minds, even if these were points of
criticism or irritation, and then pray together, often ministering to one another at the same time. Occasionally these were
very painful sessions when some home-truths would be spelt
out, ending perhaps in tears; but it was through these times
that we learnt a lot about ourselves, and the Spirit of God was
able to heal areas of our lives that needed sorting out.

In spite of the threat that we posed to some members of our
church, the obvious value of the household became impressive for several families and individuals; and after two years of
being on our own, six or seven other households emerged,
with families moving in together, or single people joining a
nuclear family, or widows, widowers, or solo parents moving
in to find a larger family to which they could belong. We spent
much of our time trying to encourage and guide them,
although some of them were not successful. There are many
pitfalls in this way of living, and there were so many principles
we were having to learn the hard way that we increasingly
discouraged enthusiastic couples in other places from following our example. Although we did not always keep rigidly to
this, we saw the wisdom of inviting a person to join us for a
'probationary period' of three to six months before they made
a more definite commitment. During that time we would all
sense whether or not that person would be suitable for this

particular way of life, which we knew was not for everyone. We also made quite clear the priorities of household living. First, everyone must support the ministry of that house, which in our case included several growing ministries in St. Michael's, as well as my own wider work. Second, everyone must support the children, and see them as young but vital members of the household. Third, everyone must support one another, expressing this by serving each other in practical and specific ways. Then, if there was any energy left, they could look after their own interests!

The experience, which lasted for several years in York, was frankly mixed, with much pain. But through it all, quite a few people were significantly healed in various areas of their lives, the sense of fellowship within the whole congregation considerably deepened, money and possessions were much more readily shared, and several new and fruitful ministries within the church were created. For about five years, when these households were in existence, we were aware of God's presence among us in unusual ways, and many visitors to our church from all over the world spoke spontaneously about the striking quality of love and joy that they experienced within the whole congregation. Although most of these visitors spoke warmly about the worship, preaching, or whatever, the most impressive factor mentioned again and again was the experience of the living Body of Christ. We ourselves at that time might have been most conscious of pain and tears; but through our own profound and felt weakness, the grace of God was even more clearly seen.

A friend of mine, Ken Gullickson, pastor of The Vineyard, Whittier, Los Angeles, once said that our ability to minister is most effective through brokenness, when we are weak, vulnerable and hurting. This creates, he said, a sensitivity to the voice of God and to the needs of others. Nobody wants naturally to be 'weak, vulnerable and hurting'. However, it is in the opening of our lives to one another, as well as to the Lord, that this is often effected. Naturally we all like to be strong, self-confident and self-contained. It was our experience through household living especially, as well as in other ways of course, that God broke our natural strength and made us extremely vulnerable; and in this way, *his* life and joy were manifested – which others were quick to appreciate. When, through our hurts, we pulled back from this vulnerability and closed our hearts a little to each other (and to God as well) because of the pain of it all, the sense of God's presence among us was not so obvious. If we want to know 'the power of Christ's resurrection' in our midst, we must also be willing to accept 'the fellowship of his sufferings' (Phil. 3:10).

To begin with in our household, everyone paid what they could. Some paid nothing at all, since they had nothing to offer; others, with reasonable salaries as a nurse or a teacher (nothing much to shout about admittedly!), gave more than was necessary for their own keep. In this way we were able to support those who had no other means of support. When two other friends joined us, however, they gently challenged Anne and me about the question of finance. If we were really trying to share our lives together, why not share our money as well, to the extent of no one having a private bank account of his own. Instead we could have a 'common purse', a household account, into which all earnings went, and out of which everyone received exactly the same pocket money. From this, we would have to buy all our clothes, presents (for birthdays and Christmas), and other personal items, such as chocolates, perfumes, or little luxuries. It seemed a natural extension of our lifestyle, and we shared the idea with our bank manager, who was puzzled, slightly impressed (I think) and encouraging. For several years we worked on this principle, and it became a vital means of release, for me at any rate, from the constant desire to possess. Covetousness is perhaps our greatest sin, and also the root of all evil. Community living is not the only way to guard against this, of course, but it proved extremely helpful for many of us adopting this way of life.

Our children had more limited pocket money, but the rest of us received £3 a week, out of which we had to get everything that was not supplied by the household account as basic necessities for life. This meant that I started hunting round Oxfam shops for clothes, which for a rector in his early forties was perhaps a bit unusual. I picked up a few marvellous bargains, some of which I am still using. Otherwise it meant saving up for weeks before buying a pair of shoes. It also meant choosing presents with great care, and those who had time would make their own Christmas and birthday presents, trusting the inspiration of the Spirit, often with much greater satisfaction all round than going into a shop and buying something extremely expensive and possibly unwanted by the recipient. We also tried to eat less, to buy in bulk and choose carefully. We cut out altogether the expense of meals in restaurants, and learnt to celebrate birthdays and festivals at home. These were often marvellous occasions. It is surprising how creative a small community can be!

At the same time, we attempted in some small measure (and we knew that it was only a pathetic gesture) to identify ourselves with the poor in this world. We gave a lot of money for the relief of the poor and for the work of the Church. We were also able, through this shared life and common purse, to release several members of the household for full-time work in St. Michael's. For some time there were only three wage earners in our house, including me, but five full-time workers in the church, entirely supported by the household. Without this means of support, some of the most significant developments in and from the church, which I shall describe in the next two chapters, might never have come into being. For several years there were more than thirty full-time workers in the church, many of them living simply by sharing in these small communities. Some of these workers were developing new ministries; others were lay-pastors, secretaries, youth workers and so forth. In other words, the households, beginning with our own, rapidly became the facilitating ministries that Anne had foreseen, benefiting not only St. Michael's, but the wider Church too.

Naturally there were real problems. Our respective parents found it difficult visiting us in such a full house, and hard sharing us with so many others, as the congregation had also experienced. Our Christmas gifts for them, too, were a little meagre to begin with, compared with previous years, until we started to think through the continued importance of family relationships. Our children responded well to all the new additions to the family, but initially we made the mistake of having too many disturbed people in our home at one time. Indeed, many believe it to be a basic principle that you should have no really disturbed person in your house, if you can help it, when your children are under twelve years of age, as ours were. Thus the time we spent on other members of our house began to tell on our children; and one day my son's grand-father saw him put a few pennies into a box. 'What are you doing with those?' he asked. Guy replied, 'I'm saving up enough money so that we can buy a house where Mummy, Daddy, Fiona and I can live *by ourselves*!' It was amusing, and yet that little remark touched our hearts, and the message got through. However, there were obvious benefits, too. It was other members of our household who gave Fiona some musical skills, and who encouraged her in her work, particularly maths, physics and chemistry, which she is now doing for her A levels. It was others who helped Guy with practical projects in our workshop, and assisted him with his home-work. The sharing of our lives with others was by no means all negative, even as far as our family was concerned. I suspect, too, that both our children learnt to relate to others better as a result.

The most serious tensions came in our own marriage. We nearly did not make it at all; and it took us some time before we found anything like the right balance between the special relationship within marriage, and the strong brother–sister relationships we were trying to deepen within the household. Not a few crises developed, and it really seemed that our marriage would fall apart altogether on several occasions. I felt torn in various directions, and began to suffer from quite deep depression, which has afflicted me from time to time since then. None of these problems can be blamed on the 'community lifestyle', but only on the sin in our own hearts. It was especially painful for me (and I suspect for others too) to find that sin was such a reality and not just a theological issue, and that, for all my supposed spiritual maturity, I was as weak as any other person, but for the grace of God.

Miraculously God's grace won through. After numerous agonising experiences, and with the wise, patient counsel of some good friends, especially David and Jean Smith (elders in our church), Anne and I came through to a richer and deeper relationship than we had ever known since our wedding. Once we had passed through such storms, when everything seemed to be collapsing around our ears, we discovered a new and stronger commitment than we had ever known before. We learnt to be much more open to one another, sharing quickly anything that might cause unspoken tensions. Although our eight years in an extended household were sometimes incredibly painful, we now see that, through the tears, God was refining and healing us, and we have both been enriched by that testing time. Also, they were years of such fruitfulness, both in the lives of many individuals and in the life of the church, that I am sure we would do it all over again. It was a period of humbling and chastening, and vital lessons were learnt that I doubt I could have known in any other way; and both Anne and I feel we have become more whole people as a result. We are therefore immensely grateful to all those who shared with us over the years: for loving us, forgiving us, correcting us, being patient with us, and revealing to us something more of Christ. In its own peculiar way, it was perhaps the most important period of our life.

Part of the difficulty of this lifestyle is that you feel as though you are living in a shop-window. When there are problems, everyone knows about them immediately. Those who remained cautious, if not critical of the extended households used to say, 'When you think of households, you think of problems!' But there are often just as many problems within nuclear families (see the enormous tragedy of broken homes today), but not everyone knows about them in the early stages. It all takes place behind closed doors. In an extended household, however, you have to be open since there is not much that you can hide. 'It is not convenient,' said a friend of mine, 'but it is fruitful!' Throughout those years of living in this way, I discovered a quality and depth of relationships in Christ beyond anything I had ever known before. I still have a profound love for all those who lived with us, and I shall always feel a family affinity with them beyond the ordinary levels of Christian fellowship.

Together with moments of great pain, we also had plenty of fun and great joy. We joined together in Israeli dances on the rectory lawn; we went to the sea together and walked on the Yorkshire Moors together. Even the animals felt part of our life: we had a cat, a dog, a rabbit and two budgies! When a bishop came to preach in St. Michael's he joined us for tea in the rectory first. We left him to finish his sermon while most of us went off to church to prepare for the service. When the Bishop went upstairs to go to the bathroom our dog Sam protested noisily. Sam could look alarmingly fierce; so the Bishop fled from the house, accidentally dropping his sermon notes in the process. Fortunately they were discovered before he got into the pulpit.

The rich sharing of lives together in Christ is what I remember most clearly about those years of extended household living. The apostle Paul once wrote to those at Thessalonica, 'We loved you dearly – so dearly that we gave you not only God's message, but our own lives too' (I Thess. 2:8, Living Bible). Such sentiments became a living reality during those years.

Jeff Schiffmeyer, the present rector of the Church of the Redeemer, Houston, Texas, once said that 'the effectiveness of our ministry depends on the fervency of our love for one another'. The experience of shared relationships in Christ proved exceptionally creative in the life of our church, and from this stemmed a number of strategic ministries that God, in his mercy and grace, has used in various parts of the world.

13

Creative Arts

I had been at a student leaders' conference for four days, and my mind was beginning to reel with all the talking and studying that we had done. Intellectually it had been valuable, but spiritually I was feeling distinctly dry, and it was obvious that I was not the only one. I approached the leader of the conference: 'We've been here for four days, and yet we haven't once really worshipped God.' He readily agreed, and announced that there would be half an hour of hymn singing before the next session. My heart sank! Yet that had been my own perspective for many years: worship had been that bit of the service that comes before the sermon – a few hymns and psalms and prayers. My understanding of the nature of worship was minimal.

Gradually I saw the significance of the truth that worship is our primary calling. The chief end of man is 'to glorify God and to enjoy him for ever', as the Westminster Catechism expressed it. The difficulty was how, in practical ways, to develop worship so that it became the most important part of our life as a local church. Our first seven years in York were limited by an organist who was totally reliable and faithful, but did not really comprehend the spiritual aims that we were pursuing. When he left, he was replaced for a short time by a brilliant organist who was absolutely committed to Christ, but who was musically too sophisticated for our congregation. He produced amazing harmonies and I found much of his playing exciting. But I could see some puzzled expressions on the faces of those who were trying to sing the straightforward tune.

I learnt then that a natural talent becomes a spiritual gift
only when it both glorifies Christ, *and* edifies the Body of
Christ. Many gifted musicians (and other artists too) have to
learn how to serve others with their gifts, and not to use the
occasion as an opportunity for self-fulfilment. It is no doubt
good for congregations to be stretched sometimes in their
musical taste, but Jesus taught his disciples to wash each
other's feet; and preachers, musicians, singers, actors, wri-
ters, architects and others all have to learn exactly the same
lesson. Unless our contribution is helping and encouraging
others, it will never be a spiritual gift, however brilliant it may
be. It becomes 'performance', not 'ministry'. The style of
worship that is especially needed today (and is all too rare) is
one marked by gentleness and simplicity.

The real start of a new dimension in worship came when I
was away in New Zealand for eight weeks. I was having a
tremendous time touring various universities with Merv and
Merla Watson, two superb musicians and singers from Canada, whose praise and worship had thrilled me during the
International Conference at Guildford two years before.
Their music also attracted many New Zealand students, and
we saw young men and women turning to Christ because they
had sensed his presence before listening to his word. At
Dunedin we held a lunch-time meeting in the Students'
Union, and it was clear from the start that a group of students
were out to wreck the whole meeting. They made a lot of
noise, and handed out anti-Christian literature that was
aggressive and obscene. Through Merv and Merla's continued praise, however, they quietened down considerably,
and after I had been speaking for five minutes or so, the leader
of the group turned to those who were still talking and said,
'Will you shut up? I want to listen to this guy!' There was a
respectful silence for the rest of my talk, and I was able to pray
a prayer of commitment for those who were ready to receive
Christ. There was absolute stillness, and at least two students
found Christ that day.

While we were still in New Zealand, my wife back in St.
Cuthbert's brought a small group together to sing something

during one of our Family Services, simply to encourage a lay pastor who was preaching his first sermon. The group consisted of Anne, who only sometimes sings in tune, our two children (aged six and four) who played the guitar and triangle, a violinist and two others playing guitars. Significantly they were all members of our household, so that Anne's vision was again being fulfilled. Added to that, this very first 'singing group' developed out of the harmony of their lives together, not just the harmony of their music. This we later found to be a fundamental principle, which can transform any singing group or choir from a musical performance (of whatever excellence) into a spiritual ministry which brings the presence of Christ to other people. In order to back this group wholeheartedly, and to be personally identified with it, I even joined it myself for a Sunday or two, playing a borrowed guitar. I could play only three chords, and gladly stood down a week or two later when another guitarist offered his services; but the congregation loved this fresh approach to worship, and before long a more competent group was established.

Anne stayed with them for some time. Having the vision for this development in worship, she urged them to serve the congregation with their gifts, encouraged and supported the leader of the group, and stressed both the strong commitment and the sharing of lives that such a ministry demanded. All those who were willing to lead the Sunday worship in this way had to commit themselves to an evening of rehearsal each Tuesday, and, as the group became more established, the first hour of that evening was spent in prayer and in sharing together what the Lord had been saying and doing in their lives. Only as they became more open to one another in God's presence could the Spirit bind them together in God's love; and only as they learnt 'to live in such harmony with one another, in accord with Christ Jesus', could they together 'with one voice glorify the God and Father of our Lord Jesus Christ' (Romans 15:5f). Their vision was not just to sing songs, old or new, but to refresh people with the life and joy and love of Christ. Thus, this first hour on Tuesdays for prayer, praise and sharing was an indispensable part of their ministry on Sundays. Added to that they had to be willing to come about an hour early on Sundays before each service in order to pray and prepare themselves for leading in worship. Any preacher will know the importance of prayerful preparation for his sermon. Yet, if worship is the primary calling for the Christian, our preparation for worship must be equally demanding if it is not to degenerate into 'that bit before the sermon'.

Soon we discovered the necessity of a 'worship committee', which met each Monday for an hour or two (before the singing group rehearsal on the Tuesday), to plan in detail every part of the worship for the coming Sunday. Our aim was to combine the old and the new, and so to produce the appropriate blend of the more familiar hymns with the less familiar spiritual songs that were emerging. Our organist by this time was Andrew Maries, who was also an extremely gifted oboist, and again a member of our household. He was the natural leader of the singing group, and with the financial support of the household became our first full-time musical director. In this way we were able to give much more serious attention to the whole area of worship, and it has undoubtedly become one of the most essential ingredients in the life of the congregation. One Anglican nun wrote, after a visit to the church for a week: 'More than anything I am filled with thanksgiving for what I saw and heard of the worship of St. Michael's, not only in the church building, but in the whole life of the community. I came away with the impression of a Christ-centred, loving, caring and joyful community.' No worship can be taken for granted, and of course we had our ups and downs; but as we set our hearts to glorify God, so the sense of his presence in our midst touched the lives of countless people.

Being a musician, Andrew wanted to encourage other musicians in the congregation in their worship of God. This had already been done to some extent before Andrew had become our organist; but under his leadership a Family Service orchestra developed, consisting mainly of children who came regularly to that service playing their recorders,

clarinets, oboes, violins, guitars, and even a glockenspiel.
Older musicians, apart from those in the singing group, found
a regular commitment to the evening service harder, but
Andrew drew together a special orchestra for the Minster
Guest Services and other festive occasions. It was wonderful
to see more and more of the congregation, young and old
alike, taking an active part in the service instead of just sitting
in their pews.

One further expression of worship that I had not even
remotely considered was dance. I knew that the psalmist
talked often about praising God's name with dancing, and I
remembered that King David had 'danced before the Lord
with all his might'. But such Jewish exuberance in Old
Testament days was surely not for respectable Anglicans
today. Before my conversion I had loved ballroom dancing,
but afterwards I felt that dancing was one of the many things
that the good Christian did not do. So I cut it out of my life
altogether. The thought of introducing dance in any form into
worship seemed out of the question. Indeed it was never an
issue – until Merv and Merla Watson came to York, at my
invitation, bringing with them from Canada a remarkable
group of seventy musicians, singers *and dancers*, all of whom
were professionally trained. I organised two Festivals of
Praise for them in York Minster, and they were two glorious
evenings. For the first time ever I saw dance in worship, and
found it, to my surprise, quite beautiful and spiritually moving: a descant in movement. Never before had I experienced
such a majestic act of celebration. It seemed almost a glimpse
into heaven, with the glory of God filling the Minster, and I
found my spirit lifted up into exalted praise and joy. I soon
discovered that many others had been deeply affected by
those two festivals; and a group of women, of varying ages,
approached me to see if they could use our church hall to learn
how to worship God in dance. Cautiously I agreed.

To begin with, however, I had to be sure that dance in
worship was biblical. I could see plenty of references in the
Old Testament, but where was there any suggestion that
dance was a part of the New Testament Church? Was not this

a dangerous area, bringing the world right into the Church? Would not a dance group of attractive girls raise all sorts of unholy emotions in the men, no doubt including me? Surely this would detract from true worship, not add to it? Might we not be setting an unfortunate precedent or example which could lead other churches astray? These were the pressing questions which I had to face before I could possibly encourage a totally new area of worship that was virtually unheard of at that time. My information might have been limited, but I knew of no other church in the world where dance was used in worship.

As I began to study and pray, a number of pointers helped me to see the way forward. First, dance had clearly been part of the worship of God's people for many centuries before Christ; it would be strange if it suddenly ceased at the moment Jesus came to bring fullness of life and joy. Secondly, the New Testament Church used the book of psalms as their 'hymn book'; it would be strange if they sang about praising God with dancing, and never did it. Thirdly, there is no New Testament reference to the use of musical instruments in worship, yet very few Christians would question that dimension of worship. Fourthly, dance is mentioned twice by Jesus, both instances being significant. In the story of the Prodigal Son, everyone was happy when the prodigal came home, except the older brother: 'And as he came and drew near to the (father's) house, he heard music *and dancing*' – and he did not like it. On the whole it has been the 'older brother' in the Father's house who has taken exception to these 'new' forms of worship. Also, Jesus elsewhere said: 'To what then shall I compare the men of this generation . . . ? They are like children sitting in the market place calling to one another, "We piped to you, and you did not dance . . .".' Whatever we do, you respond negatively and critically.

Anne Long has put it in this way,

There are those who are very scared of anything moving in a service – either emotionally (such as the sermon) or physically (such as the kiss of peace or a dance). Some want a service that is safe and completely predictable where they can keep their liturgical masks in position and not relate to others. Certainly meeting each other in the presence of God can be very embarrassing if people are unsure about either God or each other.

That sums up much of the negative reaction to anything new in the Church today. Many Christians are not at all secure in the unchanging love of God, otherwise they would be willing for any fresh approach that sought to glorify him. Instead they try to find their security in the unchanging structures of the Church as an institution. This will always, sooner or later, quench the Spirit of God, who is the Spirit of movement.

What about unhelpful sexual emotions being stirred by watching pretty girls dance? Obviously this is a danger, and the dancers in their dress and movement must aim for modesty. But I am told, on good authority, that some women have the same sexual problems with certain preachers in the pulpit! What should those preachers do? Hide in the vestry and put their sermons on tape? Surely we must all come to terms with sexuality, since God made man in his own image, both male and female. Some men have been so afraid of sexuality that they relate very badly to women altogether. Indeed I would say that the Church in general has become almost gnostic in its attitudes to the body, treating it as though it was evil in itself. Much Western Christianity ignores the body, suppresses the emotions and concentrates almost exclusively upon the mind. But God wants our bodies to be the dwelling-place of his Holy Spirit, and it is by presenting our bodies to God that we offer him spiritual worship.

As I began to formulate these ideas, I encouraged the dancers to prepare an interpretative dance to a song of praise. Like the singing group, they met together each week, and for the first hour gave themselves to prayer and sharing from the Scriptures. It was only the quality of their relationships together in Christ that would make the dance genuinely an act of worship. None of the dancers had any professional training, although one older member had an obvious vision for this ministry and was able to help them with exercises and basic movements. Progress was soon made, and several dances were choreographed to songs of worship. I tried further to encourage the group by teaching the whole church more specifically about worship, referring to the place of dance and giving it plenty of biblical support. I also went to that first hour of prayer and sharing every week (as I did with the singing group), to demonstrate that I was with them all the way, and would give them the necessary 'covering' should any negative remarks be made.

At first, most of the congregation were as cautious about dance as I had been myself. But gradually, as we pressed on gently with it, explaining all the time what we were doing and why, this expression of worship was not only accepted but well received, and often proved a vital means of communication to the hearts of those present. One Baptist minister wrote in these words: 'I appreciated the worship very much indeed. Except that I felt like crying all the time! You ought to issue tissues at the door! One morning when I was practising being a "block of concrete", it was the dance that the Lord used to break me up and allow his Spirit to come through.' That has frequently been the comment from many people whom God has touched through dance in worship. Every area of life needs to be redeemed for Christ. Also, since God is Creator as well as Redeemer, all the creative gifts of his Spirit, such as the performing arts, can be used to his praise and glory. With this conviction we went on with the dance, despite some cautious warnings and negative criticisms, usually from those who had never seen it. I soon realised that most of these criticisms voiced fears, and I received very few negative comments once people had seen for themselves what we meant by this highly explosive word 'dance'! It was one of those times when we were sensitive to all comments and fears, but we felt it important not to be deflected from developing more effective methods of communication in this highly visual age which is largely word-resistant.

After a slow and hesitant start, dance became a natural part of our worship almost every Sunday. We also learnt a number of vivacious Israeli dances, which we performed outside the church when the weather was warm enough, and these always attracted quite a crowd of people, including tourists of many nationalities. 'What is going on?' they used to ask. 'Is it a celebration? Is it a festival? Is it a wedding?' It was the golden opportunity to say, 'Yes, we are celebrating that God is among us, and we have come to know him through Jesus Christ.' In this way, many became genuinely interested and wanted to know more, and some were undoubtedly brought to Christ – initially through the dance. During the summer months, for several years when the Spirit seemed to be with us in unusual power, we had lunch together in the church hall every Sunday, with many visitors joining us; and we would then go into a courtyard outside the hall for a time of more Israeli dancing. These proved to be wonderful community dances, and both expressed and increased our sense of oneness together in Christ. Always these spontaneous and joyful moments of celebration drew in the tourists. Although I loved to dance with everyone else (my past love for dance was being redeemed for Christ!) I spent most of the time talking to tourists about the Lord, and had the privilege of leading several to Christ – once again, initially through the dance.

As the Spirit seemed to move freely among us, it was a time of remarkable creativity. Another example of this was the making of many beautiful banners. One girl in our household had obvious artistic gifts, and we encouraged her to use them, in conjunction with several other women similarly gifted, to the glory of God. This small group spent much time in prayer and meditation on the Scriptures; and out of this, one or more of the group would have a picture in her mind for a banner. This idea would subsequently be realised, and the design of the banner often linked up with the theme of a forthcoming service. This was especially so for the great festivals in the Church year. Several banners would be hung on pillars in the church, and their dignity and beauty greatly enhanced the atmosphere of celebration, and the few words on each banner increased the sense of expectancy the moment people came into the church to worship. As more and more banners were made, it became possible to choose just the right banner for the theme of every service. Sometimes those who came with special needs would find meditating on the words and picture of a banner one of the most helpful aspects of the service.

Perhaps the most striking development of artistic gifts came in the area of drama. While leading several university missions I began to experiment with methods of communication other than just speaking. I came across one or two short dramatic readings, and at various universities asked if there were any Christian actors who could do them for me. During a mission at Oxford University in 1973 there was one student who did one of these readings brilliantly, and it made a considerable impact on all those present as well as enriching my talk that evening. His name was Paul Burbridge, and we began to strike up a personal friendship. At about the same period I was preaching in Cambridge University, and had dinner with a close and long-standing friend of Paul's, Murray Watts. We had an immensely stimulating conversation over dinner about the arts in general, and I discovered that Murray had already written one or two plays and was a dramatist with obvious potential. Moreover, both Murray and Paul had just started a street-theatre group called Breadrock, and with a group of like-minded friends spent part of their summer vacation performing their sketches – mostly enacted parables – at a seaside resort in North Wales. In this way, they were able to go among the crowds of holiday-makers and present the Gospel in attractive, humorous and lively ways that were much more readily accepted than the old-fashioned open-air evangelistic service.

Although I had not yet seen their group in action, I was fascinated by the concept, and saw the potential for marvellous communication in this generation that has been so influenced by the 'drama' of television. I could see that Christian artists today could become front-line missionaries in our modern culture, since they had learnt the language of communication for the mass of ordinary people who were right outside the Church.

I was also very much aware that Christian artists were under enormous pressure from the secular world in which they spent most of their time, and that the Church in general neither understood them nor did anything much to encourage them. The Arts Centre Group in London had been formed a few years before, and was doing excellent work in trying to reach artists for Christ, and then seeking to strengthen them in their faith; but the need for supportive churches was obvious. I wondered if in York we could perhaps start another Arts Centre Group for the north of England; and now that we had moved our main services from St. Cuthbert's to St. Michael-le-Belfrey, I wondered if St. Cuthbert's might be used for such a centre, maybe even becoming a small theatre where people like Paul and Murray could perform their plays. We spent some time thinking, talking and praying together about the possibilities.

I kept closely in touch with Paul during his time in Oxford, and when he got his degree he came as yet another member of our household to live with us for a year. We all became very fond of him, and he was a wonderful, creative member of the community. I especially enjoyed taking him with me on most of my visits to schools and universities during that year, and we had some marvellous fellowship together in Christ. He was both sensitive and caring, and his infectious sense of fun helped to release some of the tensions in the work or in the household. Even though Paul was my junior I found it extraordinarily helpful sharing closely with a Christian friend in this way, and over the years I have treasured one or two such friendships where I can be completely open and honest about my own needs, questions and problems.

Wherever we went, I would speak, and Paul would illustrate my talks with some very effective short, punchy pieces of drama. Occasionally Murray would join us. I led another mission to Oxford University in 1976, and before each talk to a packed audience in the Union Debating Chamber, Paul and Murray would perform one of their sketches. The undergraduates simply loved these. A wonderful rapport was established, with spontaneous applause at the end of each sketch.

After these sketches I found it so much easier speaking, and it
was an exceptionally profitable mission, with about 150
students finding Christ. I was increasingly excited about the
value of drama in evangelism. It had its own immediate
appeal, and cut quickly through the barriers of communication that are often huge between the Church and the world.
Of course, it is only the Spirit who can bring anyone to Christ,
but I could see the Spirit was using this method of presenting
the Gospel with considerable effect.

Paul and Murray were beginning to think seriously of
developing a theatre company, and could see that York could
be the ideal base. It had a long history of arts festivals,
including in particular the medieval mystery plays, and was
not saturated by other theatre companies as was London.
Added to that, they could see that St. Michael's could give
them the spiritual support that they would need; and indeed
the households that had been established could provide for
them financially also. This, in fact, was just what happened,
and it proved the crucial factor in everything else that followed. But for the households which supported the members
of the company in every way for the first year or two, the
venture would never have been born. Once again we saw the
vital facilitating ministry of these households, and most of the
best creative moves of the church came into being because of
them.

I was as excited by the vision that Paul and Murray were
forming as they were themselves, and gave them every
encouragement I could. In order to achieve some credibility
in the eyes of the Church for what they were about to do, both
of them went for a year to St. John's Theological College,
Nottingham, for a post-graduate diploma in theology; and it
was during that time that their vision began to unfold further.
As the original street-theatre group Breadrock they were
invited to perform a number of their sketches at the Nottingham Evangelical Anglican Congress (the Congress where I
was almost lynched by some delegates who had misunderstood my remarks about the Reformation!), and their drama
was extraordinarily well received by the large number of

Christian leaders who had gathered. Many of these leaders gave them much personal encouragement, and it became clear that their work would receive much wider Church support than just from us in York. 'Your sketches are hermeneutically sound!' said a Professor of Hermeneutics, with even a hint of enthusiasm in his remark.

During that year at St. John's, Paul and Murray, together with others from St. Michael's, joined me on one or two missions that we led in Belfast, Leeds and other places. These missions demonstrated the effectiveness of our 'multi-media' approach; and we could see that God was beginning to open up for us a sphere of ministry that was much wider than any of us had conceived.

On September 1st, 1977, after that year at St. John's, the Riding Lights Theatre Company was born. Together with Paul, the Director, and Murray, who was mainly an associate member and freelance writer, three others joined them from the start. Nigel Forde had lived in York for a number of years, and he and his wife Hilary had been converted about a year before through our church. For ten years Nigel had been a professional actor, writer and director of the Humberside Theatre, Hull, and therefore gave them just the necessary professional experience that they needed at this stage. Dick Mapletoft was another: a social worker who was a 'natural' in many of the comedy sketches, and who had the gift of quickly winning people's affection. Sarah Finch was the third, an extremely talented young actress who had recently finished her training at Manchester, possessing vitality, a marvellous voice, and unusual sensitivity for someone of her age. Two months later, an American friend working in our church, called Geoffrey Stevenson, joined them; and after several years with the company he has since become an accomplished and well-known mime-artist. Then, on January 1st, 1978, the company was completed by Diana Lang, who had taught drama at Roedean, the girls' school. Diana also had obvious talent and versatility, and was a perfect match for Sarah Finch. To begin with, all of these were living in households, apart from Nigel and Hilary Forde who had two children and a house of their own; and they all saw that their close links with our church in York were fundamental if the company were to have any spiritual ministry as well as artistic effectiveness. Paul came back to live in our own household, much to our delight, and remained with us until his marriage to Bernadette in July 1978.

During the next year or two, Riding Lights came with me everywhere, as I began to lead Christian missions, or 'festivals' as we increasingly called them, in many parts of Great Britain; and with six other talented members of my congregation, gifted in music and dance, we made many trips together. However, as the work of Riding Lights became more widely known, invitations came pouring in to them from all over this country and from abroad, and sadly I had to release them more and more from the team that I had formed for Christian festivals. I could see that a theatre company must fulfil its particular call to the theatre, and we were not able to make the best use of their time and energies on these festivals. We have always remained in very close touch, and after going through all sorts of experiences together – some exciting, some hilarious, and some very painful – our relationships became unusually deep. However, it was necessary in every way for them to develop their own work; and the wide popularity of it has been seen by the excellent sales of their books on drama (suitable for church drama groups), *Time To Act*[1] and *Lightning Sketches*[2]. Since then literally hundreds of drama groups have sprung up all over the world, some as a direct result of the vision of Riding Lights; and increasing recognition for this company has been given in the secular theatre. They won two awards for fringe theatre in the Edinburgh Festivals of 1979 and 1980, and have recently performed a full-length play for Yorkshire Television, which was well received.

Further, this means of communication has enabled them to bring the Gospel to a variety of situations: churches, cathed-

1. Hodder & Stoughton, 1979
2. Hodder & Stoughton, 1981

rals, city halls, schools, universities, shopping precincts, market-places, theatres, bars, car parks, seaside resorts, tourist centres – virtually anywhere. Drama is one of the outstanding means of presenting Christ to those who would normally have no contact with the Christian Church. At a recent mission to Oxford University (1982), and after the very positive experience of the previous mission in 1976 when Paul and Murray came to help me, the whole of Riding Lights took an active part. Each lunch-time they performed a brilliant revue in one of the colleges, which helped to dispel the false but common misconception that Christianity means a narrow form of religious piety. Then, each evening during the eight-day mission, they performed three of their sketches to illustrate the theme of my address. It was so popular that after two nights we had to move to a larger building, and an average of at least 1,000 students were present on each occasion, with many turning to Christ as a result.

As Riding Lights became less available to join me, however, I had to form another team who could travel with me. Although they were less experienced and perhaps less gifted than Riding Lights, we discovered that God was nevertheless able to use us in many unexpected ways.

14

The Mustard Seed

'Why not open a shop as part of the continuous witness of the Church in the city throughout the week?' Many of the ideas that we have are like passing dreams: they fade with the morning and are forgotten. Occasionally there will be a seminal thought which, like the tiny grain of mustard seed growing into a huge shrub, can become surprisingly influential in the kingdom of God.

Anne and I had been aware that most of the recent creative developments at St. Michael's were directly relevant for the Sunday worship; and although these were affecting the lives of a great many people, there was not much witness in the city during the week, apart from the lunch-hour service during the summer and of course the indispensable daily witness of every Christian at home and at work. We had a number of workers involved with young people, and gave strong support to a coffee bar called the Catacombs and the Detached Youth Work, both of which tried to help youngsters who were in and out of prison and often on drugs. However, God had placed us in the centre of a famous city and we were doing little to reach the tourists for Christ. We also saw the need for a centre where Christians from different churches could meet together, thus breaking down some of the barriers existing between those churches.

As a direct result of much prayer about this, we believed that God had given us a prophetic vision, if that does not sound too presumptuous, of a shop staffed by a small community of Christians from our congregation. They would live together in the same style as our own extended household, but with the specific task of serving people in the context of a restaurant and gift shop. The confirmation of this vision came from a study of Isaiah 58, and this had also been a theme at a recent parish weekend. In that chapter we read about the calling to share our bread with the hungry and to satisfy the desires of the afflicted. We also read, 'And your ancient ruins shall be rebuilt; you shall raise up the foundations of many generations; you shall be called the repairer of the breach, the restorer of streets to dwell in.' York had recently been a restored city, with much rebuilding of ancient ruins, and this, together with its history going back to A.D.71, had made it a tourist attraction. But it was difficult to 'dwell' in the city shopping centre without owning a shop. We also felt that God was calling us to encourage the spiritual restoration of the city, to match its material developments. It seemed desirable in every way to run a suitable shop where the work would be dedicated to God as an expression of his kingdom. Steadily God pressed this vision on us.

As we were praying about this, we heard unexpectedly about some premises, almost opposite St. Michael's, that could be ideal. On enquiry we discovered that the property was owned by the Church Commissioners of the Church of England, so that we could not buy it, but could rent it at a straight commercial rate. The building was in a poor state of repair, but in the heart of the city centre. We were aiming for a non-profit-making organisation (or any profit would be ploughed back into the work of the church), attempting in a gentle way to make Christ known in the city. Also the shop would be run entirely by members of the Church of England. I confess that I was disappointed that the rent was so high considering the purpose for which we wished to lease it. No doubt the Commissioners have their own responsibilities to be businesslike with the vast areas of property that they own, but I tried hard, in vain, to persuade them to reduce the rent. Considerable sums of money were also needed to put the building into working order, including the addition of stringent fire precautions, since part of the shop would be used as a restaurant. All in all it required a considerable financial commitment.

Having found the possible building for the project, the next vital task was to discover someone who would run the business and who could respond to the immediate financial needs. The idea was that they would live above the shop and lead a small community who would be willing to serve there. The members of that community, or staff, would receive their keep plus a small amount of pocket money for their personal spending. This was in line with the simplifying of lifestyle that a number in the church were attempting, and it also meant that the overheads of the shop could be kept to a necessary minimum. All this, we felt, would be one valid expression of the kingdom of God.

We clearly required a couple, therefore, who had vision and the willingness to accept a considerable sacrifice of their own. As Anne and I prayerfully pursued this further, we found the ideal couple in Philip and Wendy Wharton, who had either been converted, or come into assurance of their conversion, a few years before in the days of St. Cuthbert's. Philip worked for the National Coal Board in Doncaster; Wendy had obvious artistic flair, had worked as a buyer in a department store, and was developing evangelistic gifts. Their three children were now grown up: Judith, their daughter, was working in our home at that time, and was one of the leaders of the dance group in our congregation; Michael and David were mostly away from home. The Whartons lived in a lovely house a few miles out of York: they had a beautiful garden, which Philip especially found a source of great joy, and Wendy had made the house most attractive in every way.

As Anne and I shared our vision with them, they responded in a marvellous way. After further thought and prayer Philip and Wendy, with the total support of their family, told us that they were willing to sell their home in order to rent the property from the Church Commissioners, and pay for all the extremely expensive alterations that were necessary before they could move in. As it happened, once they had sold their house, they had to squeeze into another already full household for about nine months before the shop was ready. It was an extraordinary testing time for them all, but through much prayer and holding firm to the vision they all survived.

In May 1976 the Mustard Seed, as the shop was appropriately called because of its potential influence from small beginnings, was opened. Philip continued with his job at the Coal Board, to provide some stable income (even though they had sacrificed their property and security to make the venture possible); Wendy managed the shop; Geoffrey Stevenson, the American who was later to join Riding Lights, became the chef; and five or six girls committed themselves to serving there, four of them living above the shop in a small community with the Whartons. They began and ended each day with prayer, asking God to bring into the shop those of his choice, and praying for wisdom to know when to speak openly about Christ to the customers and when to be content simply to serve them with his love. It was extremely hard work, especially as most of the staff were actively involved in other aspects of church work, notably the dance group. Some of them also came regularly on the teams I was taking with me to lead Christian festivals in many parts of the country. Occasionally tensions would arise, as was inevitable when most of the staff were working and living in the same place, sharing their lives openly together, and often under much pressure. But visitors and customers frequently spoke about the striking atmosphere in that shop: it was so full of love and peace. Indeed, it was through the fragrance of Christ in that place, mediated through the depth of their relationships together and created through constant prayer, that many people, directly or indirectly, found the Saviour. Sometimes, after the hectic day was over, they held evangelistic supper parties for friends and business contacts; and these were some of the best that I have ever experienced.

The vision of the Mustard Seed as a meeting-place for Christians from widely different traditions was also being fulfilled. The Whartons and the staff had excellent relationships with Roman Catholic priests and nuns; the Anglican sisters from the Minster used to come regularly, and both

ministers and members of various churches used to meet over
coffee or lunch. I enjoyed the opportunity of taking journalists there for lunch, when they wanted to interview me for
some article, and always they would ask me, 'What is there
about this place? It is so friendly, and there is such a sense of
peace here!' It was natural for me to explain briefly the basis
on which the shop was created, and then go on directly to
speak about Christ. On more than one occasion I took my
guest across the road to St. Michael's after lunch and had the
privilege of leading him to Christ.

With Wendy's creative imagination, there were many other
positive aspects to the work. Members of our church with
appropriate talents made banners for sale (mostly smaller
versions of the ones we had in our church). Others designed
notepaper and an attractive mural for the shop itself. Local
craftsmen were given orders for their pottery, artists for their
paintings. There was also a good sale of books and albums,
some of which came from our fellowship. It was a venture
which involved many more than just those working at the
Mustard Seed. Anne and I felt that this was one of the most
exciting projects we had so far seen during our first eleven
years in York. In spite of some tensions in relationships,
which occur everywhere when people work and live in close
proximity, the entire work was creative and wholesome, a
marvellous expression of the kingdom of God in contempor-
ary and relevant terms. It was used for evangelism, renewal
and reconciliation – the three burdens that have been closest
to my heart for many years. Many visitors spoke warmly
about their experiences of the Mustard Seed, and increasingly
Wendy was asked to guide similar ventures in other towns and
cities. It was encouraging also to see the staff maturing
spiritually, and most of them are now active in various forms
of Christian service.

It was therefore all the more shattering three years later
when Anne and I heard, while on holiday with our children in
Cornwall, that the Mustard Seed was in danger of total
closure. We could hardly believe our ears.

The Archbishop of York, Dr. Stuart Blanch, had encouraged me to have something of a 'sabbatical' in 1979, but with our children still at school, and as I was frequently away from home on missions and festivals, we felt that the most we could do was to spend all the school holidays away as a family, and this included three weeks in a tiny cottage in Cornwall – for what turned out to be one of the wettest summers on record! A telegram arrived from Philip and Wendy asking us to ring them at once. We had grown very close to them indeed, and they knew well the pressures we were under; so for them to cable us in such a way meant that the situation, whatever it might be, was serious.

Having no telephone in the cottage, we stopped at the first call-box and got through to Philip and Wendy. Thus began the first of two lengthy calls every day for the rest of our holiday as we heard about the developments. I was tempted to fly or drive back at once (and maybe should have done so – I am still not sure), but my sense of responsibility to Anne and the children, together with the Archbishop's instructions, kept us in Cornwall. Also, my 79-year-old mother was far from well, and had to be admitted to hospital in Winchester. We knew it was important to stay in the south of England and to visit her for several days on our way home.

By the time we returned, however, the problem in York had reached the point of no return, and the Mustard Seed had all but closed. What had been one of the most fruitful and imaginative enterprises I had ever been associated with, had been virtually destroyed in one swift blow. It was almost impossible to believe.

This is not the place for recriminations, and to this day I still do not fully understand the reasons for what happened. I suspect that a number of complex factors were at work simultaneously: personal frustrations and guilt projected into open criticism; a negative attitude on the part of some towards women leaders, especially those with a strong personality; different views of spirituality beginning to emerge within the leadership; a general awareness of some of the problems in the Mustard Seed since, as with every extended household, those problems were readily observable. It is worth adding,

however, that those 'problems' seemed to me to be very little
different from those of any going concern, especially where
relationships are open and committed.

Nevertheless, the next two weeks became a nightmare. It
all seemed rather like a trial. Wendy and Philip came before
the elders, about twelve of us. We asked searching questions
and made critical comments. Some questioned the whole
vision of the Mustard Seed. Others cast doubts on its prayerful origin (though prayer had always been one of its most
significant factors). Increasingly a vote of 'no confidence' was
given. All future hopes were utterly dashed.

Even more serious, Philip and Wendy themselves were all
but destroyed through the process. Having been with them
from the start, Anne and I could feel at least something of the
incredible agony they went through for many months to
come; and even three years later, I could not pass by the
premises without feeling the profound ache of past grief in my
spirit. The stock in hand, of course, had to be sold cheaply,
and the property passed on for other purposes. Philip and
Wendy were able to stay in their flat above the shop for
another two years until they were able to buy a small house for
themselves. But they lost thousands of pounds through their
obedient response to the vision which I firmly believe the
Lord gave them. It was nothing less than a miracle of God's
grace that they were eventually able to forgive, and once
again become active members of the church which had hurt
them so much.

It never helps to apportion blame. The whole sad saga was a
vivid and painful reminder that, however 'renewed' individuals or churches may feel themselves to be, we are still
sinners, in constant need of the Lord's forgiveness, patience
and love. We still hurt one another, sometimes unbelievably
so, and still have to go on forgiving one another, as much as
seventy times seven, as Jesus taught. The message of the
Gospel is that of God's grace through human weakness; but
human sin can quench the Spirit and hinder God's work, so
that Satan, temporarily at least, appears to triumph. Philip
and Wendy had always felt it important to submit to the

recognised leadership in the church, whether they felt those leaders to be right or wrong. Through their humble submission, astonishingly painful though it was, God later blessed them both with a wider and richer ministry than before. Even the whole church eventually experienced the resurrection that follows crucifixion, when God is in control. But the crucifixion was agonisingly real.

The rise and fall of the Mustard Seed brought many of us to our knees, as we repented of all the sin and folly that made the nightmare happen. Thus began a refining, chastening process within the whole congregation, although we did not yet know that the most severe fires were still to come.

15

Shared Leadership

It was through the recognised leaders in the church that the Mustard Seed came to a sudden and tragic end. Yet whatever were the rights and wrongs in what happened (and it was difficult not to feel that we had all been wrong), the shared leadership that I encouraged in St. Michael's was an indispensable part of its growth over the years.

Often I think that I lack vision (Anne is the visionary in our partnership), and usually I have been prodded into action either by Anne's prophetic insights or by murmuring within the church. I am encouraged to think that even Moses was sometimes spurred into taking a lead through the murmurings of the children of Israel. When the problems became too numerous for him, he wisely consulted his father-in-law (which suggests how serious the situation had become!) and shared his leadership in an orderly and impressive way. He had 600 leaders over thousands, 6,000 leaders over hundreds, 12,000 leaders over fifties, and 60,000 leaders over tens – making 78,600 leaders in all. That must have eased his personal responsibilities considerably, providing he was on good terms with all his leaders.

After five years in York, and with my university work around the country taking me away increasingly, some of the congregation were complaining that I was not sufficiently at home to see to all the pastoral problems in a rapidly expanding work. From 1967 onwards we had held an annual residential parish weekend away from York, and these had always been significant times for welding our congregation close together and for discerning God's direction for us in the coming year. In 1970, 126 came away for the weekend, and I put them to work in small groups to review the entire work of the church and to pray for the Spirit's guidance. Partly as a result of this, it became clear to me that I had to ask others to share in the pastoral load of the church.

In Acts 6, when there were complaints about Greek widows who were being neglected, the apostles asked the congregation to choose seven men 'of good repute, full of the Spirit and of wisdom', to help with this pastoral need. Once they reorganised in this way, we are told by Luke that 'the word of God increased'. I therefore preached about the need for others to share in the work I was doing in the church, and asked the congregation to suggest, in writing, those who might be suitable. I noted that in Acts 6 the apostles kept the right of appointment of the seven in their own hands, even though the congregation was asked to make the choice. This seemed to be a wise procedure, as I did not believe that I should opt out of the God-given responsibility that I had over the congregation as a whole. I was sharing my leadership, not dividing the authority of it into a number of equal parts. Further, before taking any action at all, I consulted with the Parochial Church Council, since that is the legally elected governing body in any local Anglican church, and they unanimously agreed with the suggested development.

Naturally I prayed much about the choice of 'elders' (as we called them), and it was greatly encouraging for me to see that the choice of the congregation exactly coincided with my own personal feelings. In October that year, six men were commissioned by the Bishop of Selby to serve as elders in the church. To begin with the appointment was only for a year, since it was obviously experimental. I had heard of one, or perhaps two, Anglican churches that had done something similar, but the whole idea in our tradition was a relatively new one. The six elders happened to include the church-wardens and readers, but there was no automatic or 'ex officio' qualification. At that time, I was still a curate, and therefore could not have another clergyman to assist me in the growing work. Thus I had to call in the support of laymen to take on some of the burden of pastoral leadership. We met regularly together, once every two weeks in those early days, and I found this group immensely supportive.

Although Anne totally agreed with this new move, the practical implications of it all were painful for her. Up to this point, in spite of many strains, Anne and I together had been the effective leaders of the work, as we tried to discern God's guidance for each new stage of development. Now that the elders had come into being (and for many years they were strictly all men), Anne was excluded from this leadership group. She therefore had to work indirectly through me, trying to impart through my thick skin some of the creative ideas that she was constantly having; and then I had to work them out for myself before sharing them with the elders. In the first-century Church in Antioch, the leadership of the congregation consisted of a group of prophets and teachers. On reflection, it was ridiculous that we should have excluded for many years the one person who had such a growing prophetic ministry. Indeed it would have been most healthy if that prophetic ministry could first have been exercised within the eldership. But our prejudice against women leaders was strong, and the thought of Anne, or any other woman, joining that group never even entered our heads. An official report on our church by the Archbishops' Council on Evangelism (a most thorough report that was extremely searching and helpful) commented about our fellowship: 'It is male-administered, female-attended, mother-and-family and student orientated . . . It is directed by men, women being excluded from the eldership, but playing a leading role through prophecy. There is a real danger of compromising prophetic vision where it does not tally with the going concerns of the eldership. A determined individualist would find the whole set-up frustrating.' I did not realise at the time just how frustrated Anne and several others would find the male domination that had emerged from this otherwise necessary move.

In spite of all that, the experiment was clearly successful, and the elders were subsequently appointed for three years at a time, subject to reappointment. This allowed within the eldership a certain turnover, determined partly by age, health and other commitments. We were always on the lookout for those whose primary ministry was pastoral. The Church Council was the governing body within the church, and therefore its main function was administrative; but it happened that most of the elders were also on the Council so that there was never any friction between the two groups. The Council met only five or six times a year, but the elders were soon meeting every Saturday at 7 a.m., and about every six weeks we spent the whole of Saturday morning together (later we met at 6.30 a.m. each Tuesday). I was quite certain that the Council as a whole had no desire for that demanding commitment! In Anglican terms, the eldership was virtually the pastoral subcommittee of the Church Council, but that was a clumsy title and it was never used. Always the elders were commissioned by the Bishop of Selby or the Archbishop of York, so that we tried to bring the whole scheme under the authority of the wider Church. In effect, the commissioning of the elders was a local ordination for ministry within our church.

In July 1972 we went one stage further, and one of the elders, Peter Hodgson, was commissioned as a full-time Lay Pastor. Peter had been licensed as a Reader for some twenty years, and while running his own radio and television servicing business had enjoyed increasing conversations about Christ in the homes where he went on business. Our task as a Church Council was simply to recognise the obvious pastoral gifts that God had given him, to hear his own sense of calling to full-time service within the church, and then to commission him for that purpose, accepting the financial responsibilities of a married man with a wife and three growing children. Peter was an invaluable helper since he had lived in the area all his life, and knew intimately some of the needs of those who came to us.

One almost impossible task facing the elders was to put a brake on my own outside engagements. I was slowly learning

to say 'no' to invitations, but too quickly responded to
opportunities both for evangelism (especially) and also for
the renewal of the Church. Some invitations I refused with
minimal thought; but the others I brought to the elders'
meetings, and perhaps a disproportionate amount of time was
spent sifting through those invitations to see how I should
reply. However, for me it was immensely helpful submitting
to the combined wisdom of the elders; and since one of them
was my doctor, Walter Stockdale, who looked after my
asthmatic problems with great care and skill for many years,
they had good reason for trying to prevent me from doing too
much. Further, since my outside engagements often increased the tensions at home, the elders had a primary
pastoral duty to perform towards us – which was not always
easy for them.

Even with the establishment of elders, which greatly eased
the pastoral load from my own shoulders, we heard further
murmurings after a year or two. The congregation was growing too big, especially after our move into St. Michael-le-
Belfrey in 1973. It was hard for people to know one another in
any depth; and, more than ever today, most people need to
belong to a relatively small and identifiable group. Our
Thursday fellowship, which had moved out of the rectory into
St. Cuthbert's, had levelled off at about 150 or more, which
was still far too big for any intimate fellowship. Consequently,
a few small groups had formed spontaneously so that people
could enjoy more relaxed fellowship within the informal
atmosphere of individual homes. The time had come, however, to organise these groups in a more structured way;
and a half-day parish conference one Saturday confirmed the
widespread desire for this to happen as soon as possible.

One area that needed immediate strengthening was the
young people's group. So in April 1973 I went to see the
Archbishop of York, Dr. Donald Coggan, to ask if I could
have a curate. 'But you are only a curate yourself!' he replied.
'Are you asking to be made a vicar?' I detected a slight
twinkle in his eye, so I dutifully and accurately answered,
'Well, I have been a curate for fourteen years, and I just

thought that perhaps . . .' The Archbishop was very gracious. On September 19th, the day of our wedding anniversary, I was instituted as vicar of St. Michael-le-Belfrey, and four days later my first curate, Andrew Cornes, joined me. I had been used by God to help Andrew find Christ at Oxford University, and I had subsequently come to respect Andrew immensely during his placement with us, as part of his training for ordination. He had an astute mind, obvious drive, gifts of leadership, and showed all the marks of becoming an outstanding preacher and teacher. Added to that his Christian experience at the camps that I had attended gave him excellent training to develop the youth work almost from scratch. One particular problem, however, had to be worked through with honesty. Andrew could not identify with the charismatic renewal, as it was now commonly called. However, my burden was already growing for the reconciling of Christians over this issue; and since Andrew's teaching was crystal clear about the heart of the biblical Gospel which I constantly sought to proclaim, I felt that it might be good deliberately to invite, as curate, someone who was definitely not a 'card-carrying charismatic', partly to demonstrate that our unity is always in Christ, and not in any particular spiritual experience.

As it happened, Andrew had three marvellous years with us. Immediately he was loved by everyone, and his gifts widely appreciated. His sermons were a model of careful and spiritual exposition, his sense of humour was infectious, his concern for individuals was full of the compassion of Christ, and, above all, his pioneer work among young people was brilliantly effective. Not only did many young people find Christ through Andrew's ministry, but his follow-up system, based largely on what he had learnt at those boys' camps, enabled them to grow rapidly in the faith. Each young Christian was attached to a family (which helped to bridge some of the generation gap), and the father or mother of that family would spend an hour a week reading the Bible with the young Christian, as well as extending hospitality through meals. By the end of those three years, the young people's fellowship, called 'Eureka' (meaning 'I've found it – or him') had grown from nothing to about 140, most of whom were steadily maturing in their faith.

In 1976 Andrew left to become Director of Training at All Souls, Langham Place. I am not sure that he changed his views about charismatic renewal as such during his time with us; but he was totally loyal, and our relationship was always one of the utmost harmony and mutual respect. Andrew was replaced by Patrick Whitworth, who had also found Christ during a time I spent at Oxford University; and Patrick took on the excellent work that Andrew had established as well as becoming more widely involved in the whole church. Andrew had spent about ninety-five per cent of his time with young people, since I saw that as a priority; but I was concerned that Patrick should receive more general training, and it soon became obvious that God had gifted him in both evangelism and teaching. It was a joy to share these aspects of the ministry with him; and once again he was much loved by the whole congregation.

The young people's group was not the only one developed at this stage. We saw that most people wanted, and needed, to belong to a small group (the ideal number being about twelve) where they could get to know one another informally. We therefore divided the regular congregation into more than twenty *area groups*, as we called them, since the determining factor for almost all of them was a geographical one. We wanted these groups to build up a sense of community in a given small area, with the opportunity of establishing good relationships 'seven days a week'. For example, although the focal point was a meeting in someone's home every other week, for the purpose of praise, prayer, study, sharing and ministry, we wanted the relationships in each group to become much deeper than that. It was a natural practice in our group for members to walk in and out of each other's homes without needing to knock or ring the door bell. If the visitor saw a young mother struggling with washing, cooking and babies, immediate practical help might be offered, followed by a helpful chat over a cup of tea and then specific prayer.

Mothers with very new babies found that all their meals were provided for them and often their other children were looked after, sometimes staying in the homes of nearby families. There was also much sharing of property such as cars, washing-machines, lawn-mowers. Two women in one group might do a weekly shop for the whole group. Offers for baby-sitting would frequently be made, and meals cooked for any who were ill. We wanted to encourage the sharing of the whole of our lives, not just Bible study and prayer. Some people could not come to regular meetings, but they were still important members of the 'community of God's people' in that area, and we wanted as many as possible to feel that they belonged.

Each area group had its leader, and ideally an assistant leader too, since it was our hope (not always realised) that if these groups grew healthily they should be willing to split, multiply or 'bud' every year or two. Some groups, like individuals, were more gifted in evangelism than others, and thus tended to grow more quickly. Others were more committed to ministry within the church. Sometimes the groups were encouraged along specific lines of Bible study, and a number of them had particular prayer projects, such as the support of certain missionaries. But all groups were designed for the sharing of lives. Normally this 'sharing' would consist of personal thoughts drawn from the Scriptures, but occasionally it would emerge from the ordinary events of life. We knew that God is always trying to speak to us, through his word but also through every circumstance of life, and we encouraged each other to listen to God, to hear what he was saying and then to share it with one another. In this, it was important to be open and honest, so that within the small group of committed Christians there could be freedom to mention quite personal needs, thus drawing out the love, prayer and support of others in the group. It was in 'speaking the truth in love' that we were trying to grow up into Christ in every way.

Another vital aim of these groups was pastoral. When needs of any kind arose – and they were always doing so of course – the members of the group (not necessarily the

leaders) tried to help one another in spiritual or practical
terms. Further, each elder had the oversight of two or more of
the groups, so that if the pastoral need lay beyond the
combined experience of the group, it was passed on to the elder.
And then, if that elder felt inadequate to deal with the
problem, he could, with permission, share that need with
another elder of greater experience. In this way, it was
obvious that the pastoral load of the church was being borne
by a growing number of men and women, thus easing the
enormous strain that any clergyman will feel when his congregation is increasing in size.

   All the elders, by virtue of their living in some area, were
members of an area group, as well as having responsibility for
one òr more others; but they were never leaders of those
groups, except in emergency, so as to encourage more and
more lay-leadership within the church. On one snowy occasion, when I was present at my own area group, a young wife
apologised that her husband had been delayed from work
because of the snow, and she explained that he should have
been the leader for that night. 'Oh well,' she said, 'I suppose
that I had better lead it instead of Colin.' I was delighted that
she did not think of handing the group over to me, even
though I was the only clergyman present. Moreover she led it
extraordinarily well, and I was greatly refreshed by the whole
evening.

   Group leadership is a skilled and demanding role, and very
few of our leaders were naturally gifted in this. We later
developed, therefore, a number of 'support groups', consisting of two or three elders together with the various area group
leaders for which they were responsible; and these support
groups met every two or three weeks. They also were expected to share their lives together, since the way in which
they did this, in a group of leaders, would be likely to
determine the quality of the area groups which they were
leading. Also, of course, they were able to raise difficulties
they were experiencing within their groups, or share certain
aspects that they had found valuable; and then they prayed
for one another. As with every structure like this, some

groups went better than others, and no system is perfect. But the sense of fellowship within the whole congregation grew almost visibly as a result, and the individual needs of the majority had much more chance of being met than if the whole work depended on the feverish activities of one or two hard-pressed clergymen.

It is significant that virtually every major movement for spiritual renewal in the history of the Church has been marked by the development of the small group. The amazing missionary impact of the Moravians lay in their constant attention to relationships, based on small groups. John Wesley, who largely owed his conversion and evangelistic zeal to the Moravians, organised his 'class-meetings' or 'nurture cells', and these became a vital part of the extraordinary influence he had on the whole of England in his day. The remarkable growth of the Pentecostal Church in South America is also due, in part, to the emphasis on the cell structure. Numerous other illustrations can be given. Naturally there are dangers. Unless the leaders develop close relationships with one another, these groups can become independent or divisive. Unless the groups see that part of their function is evangelism and service, they can degenerate into unhealthy introspection. Unless the members of the group develop friendships outside the church altogether, the groups can tragically become safe and comfortable religious ghettos, useless as a witness to the wider world. Unless there is constant training and encouraging of leaders, some groups will soon die a natural death. Yet, given these and other areas of concern, the sharing of leadership became an indispensable part of the growth and witness of St. Michael's Church.

Even this degree of shared leadership, however, was not enough for the growing work. Throughout the seventies, my ministry had been steadily widening to various parts of Great Britain and to other countries in the world, and I found it increasingly hard to cope adequately with the demands in York as well. The wider ministry seemed to have the backing of church leaders of most denominations, and we could see that God was using our Christian missions and festivals in many towns and cities; but I could not sustain the pressure indefinitely. My health was not good: my asthmatic attacks required frequent courses of steroids. And the travelling work always imposed strain on our family relationships. It was clearly not easy for Anne, nor was it much easier for me.

We had invited the Archbishops' Council on Evangelism to study our parish in depth and to make a detailed report on their observations, and in November 1977 a team of nine spent a week with us all. They studied our worship and prayer life, our evangelism and pastoral care. They looked into our finances and practical administration. They examined our preaching and teaching, our work among children, young people and students. They spent time in our households, and asked searching questions about the area groups, the creative arts groups and methods of communication. Every aspect of the work was carefully researched. Most of the comments were exceedingly encouraging. Concerning the creative arts, for example, they stressed that 'man does not learn by words alone'. They commented that

> there are so few congregations as free to experiment in these forms, yet dance, movement and drama are the very warp and woof of the TV age, the media whereby most adult public communication now takes place . . . Most important of all, since the subject here is the communication of Christ to the world today, the team pleaded for the continued examination of the most effective blendings of dance, music, movement, drama, participation in liturgical prayer, and preaching and everyday witness *as expressions of the Word within the Body of Christ.*

Helpfully, the team also revealed a number of weaknesses in our church life which needed immediate attention.

It was hard not to feel threatened by the exercise, and yet we all knew that it was extremely healthy for us to be 'examined' in this way, especially as so many visitors were coming to learn from us. During the week I talked with Canon John Poulton, the leader of the team, and he made a suggestion that was exactly in line with what I had been thinking. 'Why not bring in someone as vicar, to run St. Michael's under your overall leadership, while you become rector, with a greater freedom for travelling?' I had already considered this seriously as a possible solution, so this extra confirmation was just what I needed. I knew that a slightly similar arrangement had worked with John Stott at All Souls, when Michael Baughen went there, so at least the idea had a precedent.

The question was, who should become vicar? If a newcomer came in, it might be years before he gained the confidence of the congregation, and I knew of no one who was an obvious choice from outside York. However, we had a young clergyman in our congregation, who was a travelling secretary with the Church Pastoral Aid Society, Graham Cray; and increasingly Anne and I felt that he might be exactly the right person. He was already an elder of our church in his own right, and he and his supportive wife Jackie were thoroughly accepted and liked by all in the congregation who knew them. As part of the week with the Archbishop's Council on Evangelism, we had a residential weekend with our elders and Church Council members; and during that time Anne and I talked to Graham and Jackie at length about the ideas that were beginning to form in our minds. They were somewhat overwhelmed at first, but warmed positively to the idea, and it became obvious to us that they shared our vision for the church exactly, as well as being able to introduce some fresh and helpful elements. I discussed all this with the elders the next day, and it seemed right to approach the Archbishop, Dr. Stuart Blanch, for his advice.

It so happened that the Archbishop was due to preach two weeks later, and I had an opportunity on that evening to raise the issue with him. Immediately he saw the value of the scheme; and so plans were put into action, and on July 1st, 1978 Graham began work as vicar of St. Michael's, the official service being conducted by the Bishop of Selby on July 20th. Thus began a wonderful relationship between Graham, Jackie, Anne and myself, as we shared together the primary role of leadership in the church. It seemed as if an immense

16

Tensions and Division

The three common stages of any community are *honeymoon*, *nightmare* and then *reality*. Much the same is true also of a new ministry in a church. To begin with, the congregation were overjoyed with our new arrangement. The fresh depths of Graham Cray's teaching touched many people's lives; his constant presence in York was a refreshing change from my increasing absence; and a variety of loose ends in the church were beginning to be tied up. It was largely through Graham's initiative that the area groups were reorganised into manageable sizes, and support groups for the leaders came into being. Time and again I was impressed by his mature grasp of the pastoral needs in the church, and he was clearly a gifted counsellor – a fact that many came to appreciate for themselves in the following months.

Nevertheless, the changeover of leadership is a time when various negatives come into the light, particularly any frustrations and criticisms which might have been suppressed out of deference to the previous leader. After a year or so, I became aware of new influences from one or two leaders (not Graham) beginning to creep in, which were pulling the church in a different direction. Graham was aware of this as well, but I was not always around to support him. There were some severe prophecies about God's judgment on our church, and these instilled an unhealthy fear and critical spirit into parts of the congregation. I personally questioned whether those prophecies were from the Lord; but, significantly perhaps, they were all given when I was away, and I heard only a recording or report of them when it was too late to do much about them. The boat was beginning to rock, and the storm was still only on the horizon.

A little later, I heard that a number within the church were quietly visiting a non-denominational fellowship in Northern Ireland, and going back there on several other visits, taking their friends with them. There was nothing wrong about this in itself. Indeed, many from throughout Northern Ireland had visited our church on several occasions, and apparently were blessed by those visits. But then I discovered that a small group in our church were putting themselves under the authority of the leaders of that Ulster fellowship, and their leaders, in turn, were coming under the authority of other leaders in Florida, U.S.A. They were apparently looking for a much stronger authority structure, involving more rigid discipling, shepherding and submission. Moreover this group in our church were advocating a slightly different aspect of spirituality, which had all the dangers of becoming a super-spirituality, and they were questioning the developments of the creative arts within the church, which God had been using with much obvious blessing.

It was possibly due to these emphases that an investigation was held into Anne's ministry. One or two elders felt that she had been too strong and dogmatic, which, if true at all, was doubtless due to her having spiritual maturity and vision beyond that of most of the elders – particularly frustrating, since she was a woman with no voice in the eldership. Up to that point Anne had been a much valued leader of the area group and area fellowship (a larger body comprising about six area groups), a prominent member of the worship committee for years, and the founder-leader of the Children's Workshop – an exciting and creative group treating children as members of the Body of Christ and encouraging them, at their own level, to take a full part in the life of the church. Anne had also initiated a number of women's groups, which had proved an enormous support for many women, some of whom were under much pressure domestically.

The result of the investigation was that Anne was required

by the elders to leave *all* the groups in which she had been involved, without exception, for a period of six months at least – although it was difficult to see how she could go back into them after that time. Part of the reason given was to strengthen our own marriage relationship, which actually had been steadily improving at that stage; but since I was shortly to go off to Australia and New Zealand for ten weeks (almost half those six months), the decision was pastorally disastrous. In spite of a vigorous protest from both Graham and me, the recommendation somehow went through, and for Anne the spiritual and emotional effect was like an amputation of both her arms and legs. It was exceedingly traumatic, although I was amazed to see how well, after an initial struggle, she managed to accept it, since she always determined to submit to the elders whether she felt that they were right or wrong. I was far more angry than she. I wrote a furious letter from New Zealand to one elder, and later apologised for my outburst.

The tour in Australia and New Zealand was an exhausting one, though with numerous encouragements throughout. I shall always remember the best street theatre we have ever experienced, in the Cathedral Square of Christchurch. An estimated crowd of 1,000 gathered and the sense of communication was excellent. An aerial photograph of the event is certainly impressive. Likewise I shall remember our final night in Auckland where, despite my fears and misgivings, the Racecourse Grandstand was booked. I felt it was the wrong time of year: cold, dark, windy and threatening to rain. However, the confident faith of the organisers was justified: a crowd of between 6,000 and 9,000 turned up (the estimates varied), and streams of people came forward in the dark to say that they had committed their lives to Christ. Altogether in that tour I preached 150 times in fifteen different centres, and the team I went with worked equally hard – Phil and Joy Potter, Liz Attwood and Pauline Hornby, with local additions helping us out. Our final stop was in Canberra where we had packed meetings in the Big Tent directly in front of Parliament House. Imaginative publicity added to the festival, and I found myself described as a 'gentle-mannered rector' and the

team as 'energetic musicians, dancers and actors who have
leaped across the British scene with a burst of Spring Fever
which lasts all year round'. I think the spring fever was sagging
a bit by that stage, but everywhere we were startled to see how
God was using our varied presentation of the Gospel. Even in
the two most discouraging meetings (from our point of view)
we heard later how people's lives had been changed by the
Spirit of God.

My telephone calls to York each week, however, were in
sharp contrast to the blessing that we were continuously
experiencing. I found Anne to be increasingly depressed not
by her removal from all the groups to which she had given her
life, but by the tensions and splits developing in the church,
particularly within the leadership. There had been more
stringent prophecies, and one or two leaders were clearly
trying to swing things their own way. They were accepting
neither Graham's leadership, nor, by implication, my own.
Indeed, it was during my tour that I came to understand more
clearly one crucial principle in shared leadership.

In one city I met a minister who told me, after one of my
seminars: 'David, for years I have been trying to share my
leadership. But now I find that they are all pulling in different
directions.' This very fine man had been the pastor of his
church for fifteen years, and God's work there had been an
inspiration to Christians all over the country. Now, amazingly, he was experiencing just the same problems that we were
going through in York. At the next seminar we discussed in
greater depth the whole issue of shared leadership, and saw
that the main leader (vicar, minister, or pastor) has a God-
given 'apostolic' role to play, in the way that Timothy was the
apostle of the church at Ephesus. Now, shared leadership
begins with the sharing of lives and building up deep relationships of love, commitment and trust. Unless that quality
of relationship exists, shared leadership is fraught with dangers through the spirit of competition and self-seeking. But
even when the fusion of lives has genuinely taken place, there
must still be the leader of leaders, and others must respect
that God-given call. The other leaders may, in love, question,

challenge or even rebuke if necessary; but they must, in the
long run, submit to the one who is over them in the Lord. The
tragedy of the Church today, not least in 'renewal circles', is
that 'every man does what is right in his own eyes' – which was
the mark of spiritual degeneracy in the Old Testament, and
the sign of carnality in the New.

On my return from Australia, I found our church more like
the Corinthian Church than at any other time during the
previous fifteen years. At Corinth, various factions formed
round the different personalities of Paul, Apollos and Peter.
This was tragic, wrote Paul, since those leaders were only
servants through whom God worked to bring life to others.
They were nothing in themselves. Moreover, he said, the one
and only foundation for any church is Jesus Christ; it can
never be the personality, gifts or even teaching of a particular
leader. Paul went on to say that it is therefore extremely
important how we build on that one foundation of Christ. The
whole theme of the chapter (I Cor. 3) is that of the unity of the
Church, so that if we build up anything which becomes
divisive, we are building with 'wood, hay, straw' – materials
which will not stand the fiery test of God's judgment. Indeed,
if anyone destroys the temple of God, God will destroy him.
Paul could not have been more emphatic about the sinfulness
of divisions within the Church.

I had one brief day off after my ten-week tour, recovering
from jet-lag and total exhaustion, before plunging into a
number of intense meetings and discussions as we tried our
utmost to avoid a split. However the splinter group, as it was
rapidly becoming, was preaching a dangerous idea, currently
taught in some circles but with no theological basis, a distinc-
tion between the *logos* and *rhēma* of God (both words being
used interchangeably in the New Testament for the word of
God). They held that the *logos* referred only to the general
word of God in the Scriptures; but the *rhēma* was the prophetic
word, God's word for now. Further, although there may be
general agreement about the *logos* of God, our unity and
fellowship depends in practice, they claimed, on our response
to the *rhēma* of God. One of the leaders of this splinter group

wrote to me: 'Unity is not built on a relationship with my brother, but on a response to the word of God. Thus you may have as much unity as you have agreement on the *rhēma* of Jesus Christ.' If there is a disagreement in our response to the *rhēma* of the Spirit, it is virtually impossible to maintain any working fellowship. Thus, they concluded, they had no choice but to separate themselves from us.

The subtlety is that all this may sound plausible for the Christian who genuinely wants to be obedient to God, and I did not doubt the sincerity of this group. I had known them, loved them, prayed for them and worked with them for many years. The trouble was that the basis on which they felt they had to withdraw was entirely fallacious. Our unity is, quite simply, in Christ. The New Testament permits us to separate from others *only* if they deny either the divinity of Christ, his death for our sins, or his resurrection from the dead. All this we tried to explain as clearly as we could, both publicly and privately. Graham, again entirely with my support, even asked the main leader of this group to be an elder again, when the time came for the reappointment of elders. This was a final attempt to avoid division, but the invitation was not accepted.

Perhaps the final straw came when Graham gave a masterly series of four sermons on leadership and, as vicar but with my total agreement, included three women in the next body of elders, one of those women being Anne. Many of us felt that the inclusion of women was long overdue, but that particular group found this altogether unacceptable. About twenty left the church. Although we were thankful that a much larger group did not leave us (we had been told that 150 would go), the pain was still enormous, especially as we had enjoyed such close fellowship with them for many years.

Looking back, I can see that the considerable overlap between my leadership and Graham's was extraordinarily important, and but for that factor the split might have been much worse. I wonder if this should not be the pattern for the handover of the leadership in any church, especially where the previous leader has been there for a long time.

In spite of the prophecies of God's judgment upon us, the shaken and chastened congregation found a new unity in Christ, gave Graham full support once again in his role as vicar, and became hungry for further spiritual renewal. Through the visit of a gifted pastor and a great friend of mine, John Wimber (from Yorba Linda, California), we had another Pentecost. At their own expense, John brought over a team of twenty-nine from his congregation, and the Spirit of God worked through them with unusual effectiveness and power. There were some wonderful healings and conversions, and many were filled with the Spirit. Those who had recently separated themselves from us kept away; but within the rest of the congregation there was a marvellous healing of relationships where tensions still existed. John Wimber, whose own church had grown from nothing to 4,000 in four years and who has wide experience of churches in many places, told me that he had never found any other church like ours that was hurting so much. The sense of grief was acute. Because of the special depth of shared relationships that God had given us in Christ, the split had caused terrible wounds. Through this we felt, no doubt in very small measure, the pain that Christ must feel over the divisions in his Body, the Church today.

Those who leave their churches to form 'non-denominational' fellowships need to realise what they are doing. As soon as those fellowships become more structured and administer the sacraments of baptism and the Lord's Supper, they virtually become churches; and when those 'house churches' have some affiliation with one another, another denomination is born. This is the sad but constant witness of church history, but we never seem to learn the lessons of the past. Often I say to those who are impatient with the stuffiness of their traditional church: 'If you want more life, give your life; if you want more prayer, give your prayer; if you want more love, give your love . . .' It is only as the grain of wheat falls into the ground and *dies* that it will bring forth a harvest.

Significantly, when the Spirit came, in Ezekiel's vision of the valley of dry bones, he did not blow the bones away and start with something entirely new, as he could easily have done. He worked on those dry and dusty bones, bringing them together, clothing them with flesh, and instilling new life into them. This is what I see God is doing with all the denominations throughout the world today. There is often an unholy impatience when Christians divide, often on some minor issue, to do their own thing. It is worth reflecting that Jesus continued worshipping in the synagogue and Temple for some thirty years, patiently bearing with its spiritual deadness, before his incredible and brief ministry took place. The only divisions that are in any way justifiable are when Christians are literally driven out of their churches through active persecution, as with Wesley and Whitefield (though they did their utmost to remain within the Anglican Church throughout their lives), or when the institutional church has apostasised by denying the most fundamental tenets of the Christian faith. All other divisions are wrong and sinful, and they grieve the Holy Spirit of God. We need only to see the urgent apostolic appeals for unity within the New Testament epistles to understand how important this is.

If we really followed the Spirit we would be willing to go through suffering and crucifixion if need be – no doubt at the hands of religious people – in order to bring life to others. To form another church of like-minded people, thereby impoverishing the lives of our brothers and sisters who are working hard for renewal within their own churches (however slowly and imperfectly), is an easy option and not the way of Christ. Indeed, it is a sad twist that those who genuinely want to 'obey the Spirit' can so easily 'grieve the Spirit' by their actions, which are contrary to the word of God.

Naturally there were faults on our side too. No doubt we should have been more renewed, more prayerful, more committed, or whatever. In one sense this will always be true. In any painful split like this, no one can point the finger; everyone needs the mercy and forgiveness of God. We are all in the wrong. The amazing truth is, that in spite of our sinful divisions God can so overrule what we do to one another (and to him) that his kingdom grows even more. The apostle Paul once had an argument with his great friend Barnabas. Luke tells us in Acts 15 that 'there arose a sharp contention, so that they separated from each other; Barnabas took Mark with him and sailed away to Cyprus, but Paul chose Silas and departed . . .' It seems that the Church expanded still further as the result of God's mercy and grace in the midst of human sin.

17

Renewal Weeks

'Go on talking,' I said. 'I think the Lord is saying something through you.' I began to scribble notes as fast as I could. I was at the sharing time of the dance group, and one member of that group was talking quietly about her thoughts concerning possible future developments in York. As Sue talked, I sensed that what she was sharing was prophetic in its quality. That was in the summer of 1976.

During the previous three years, since our move into St. Michael-le-Belfrey, many church leaders from Great Britain and overseas had visited our church to see what we were learning about evangelism, renewal and church growth. Occasionally those visits, brief and seemingly insignificant, had resulted in the transformation of people's ministries, much to our surprise. However, although we felt it right to give time to clergy and other leaders, the same questions were being asked over and over again; and it was a time-consuming business repeating the same answers. I seemed to be available even less for my own congregation, and though the time spent with one visitor after another was nearly always profitable, the demands being made on me and on some of the other elders were proving a problem.

'Why don't we plan a special week, perhaps twice a year,' asked Sue, 'when we invite lots of leaders to our church, let them stay in the homes of the congregation, experience the life of the fellowship, and see for themselves its strengths and weaknesses, and hold seminars so that we can share what we are trying to learn?' The whole vision excited me. Not only would this concentrate our time with visitors into two main weeks in the year (apart from some exceptions for overseas visitors), but those who came could see God's work among us in much more depth than I could ever begin to explain in the course of a few hours. It had many obvious advantages; and instead of the congregation finding that much of my time was being absorbed by those outside York, they themselves would be directly involved in sharing any vision that God had given us.

The elders were enthusiastic about the idea, and two prophetic words were later given confirming that God wanted to use us as a source of encouragement and renewal for other churches. But for this initiative from the Lord (as I took it to be), I would never have dared to launch these weeks for local church renewal. Without some conviction that we were obeying the leading of the Spirit, the whole idea would have been presumptuous. Who were we to tell other churches what to do, even by implication? Those of us in the hot seat of leadership were profoundly aware of numerous weaknesses in our own congregation. We ourselves were in constant need of spiritual renewal and greater maturity. In fact, I was delighted later on when I received a letter from a Swiss pastor: 'We had heard that St. Michael-le-Belfrey was an almost perfect church. We could hardly believe it, but we praised the Lord. Now we have been to York personally, now we have seen. It is not perfect, and now we praise the Lord even more. If the Lord can use sinners such as the people in St. Michael-le-Belfrey, he can use us too!' That was clearly the good news we had to share: if God could do something among us, he could do something anywhere!

In many ways, this proved the strength of our Renewal Weeks, as we called them. The first took place in April 1977. Although we did not advertise it at all, word got round and we were inundated by bookings. We organised two a year (each April and September, for six days at a time), and held twelve in all, with some 1,500 coming from all over the United Kingdom and from many countries overseas. Most of the participants were leaders – since we always stressed that these

weeks were for that purpose – and those who came represented many traditions and denominations. The main difficulty
we had was finding sufficient hospitality to accommodate
all those who wanted to come. There was an undoubted
momentum of the Spirit, which confirmed our discernment of
God's initiative in the whole venture. Apart from those from
England, especially large numbers came from Northern Ireland, Wales and Sweden.

These weeks took a simple form, and were superbly managed by a businessman Douglas Greenfield, who was one of
our elders, and by his wife Joan. Normally guests arrived on
the Friday evening and settled into the homes where they
were staying. Some of the hosts had never received guests
before, and one or two embarrassing situations had to be
sorted out quickly. We had the occasional complaint of
impossible beds or bedroom doors that could not shut. But
other hosts were so generous in their hospitality that their
guests found this experience of loving relationships the most
refreshing part of the week. On the Saturday morning we
took time explaining some of the biblical principles behind
renewal, particularly giving an indication as to what the guests
might expect in the Sunday services, since our developments
in terms of music, dance and drama would have been quite
new, if not revolutionary, for some of them. On Saturday
evening we usually had an entertainment, often led by Riding
Lights and supported by others in the church, to show that we
were not desperately intense and pious, but knew how to
laugh and enjoy ourselves in God's presence. This frequently
relaxed the more nervous guests who were anxious lest they
had come into a wild spiritual hot-house!

The Sunday services were always times of special joy.
When you add 100–150 leaders, all hungry for spiritual
renewal, to an already packed church, the sense of anticipa-
tion is considerably heightened. Both the Family Service in
the morning and the evening service of Holy Communion
were invariably times of unusual blessing, and helped to put
into some clear context the teaching of the seminars during
the next few days. One couple expressed it in this way,

although we had numerous similar letters from most of the participants: 'We praise our living Lord that his Spirit was so powerfully evident in the praise and worship, and in the overflowing love of the fellowship. Since coming home, we have wept together in the joy of the Spirit, and for someone who is not given to weeping, like so many men, that can only be of God!' For most people, these weeks were primarily times of personal renewal, which of course is a necessary prelude to local church renewal; and often the Spirit of God touched our visitors deeply through the worship of his people. It was not uncommon to see some, including strong and mature men, in tears. The services provided a visible and tangible expression of what we were talking about, even though later in the week we touched on numerous aspects of renewal and evangelism that were not immediately obvious in the services.

From Monday to Thursday, we met together each morning for worship and teaching, followed by a choice of seminars, covering subjects such as ministry, healing, evangelism, small groups, music, dance, drama, creative arts, youth work, counselling, children's work, catering. A team of helpers organised lunches each day, and this was so carefully and beautifully done that often it made an impression of its own, indicating that renewal touched every area of our lives, not just singing choruses! The Bishop of Selby, Morris Maddocks, came to most of the weeks, and gave an excellent seminar on healing, which was followed by the ministry of the laying on of hands, with the elders assisting the Bishop in this, and most of the guests came up for prayer. We became aware of the deep personal needs that most Christian leaders have; but who can minister to them in their churches? Where do they find for themselves the counselling that they so frequently give to others? Those healing seminars, together with many other opportunities for personal counselling, became a vital part of these weeks. Further, the presence of the Bishop also helped the guests to see the approval of the wider Church for these weeks, and indeed bishops from elsewhere were even sending their clergy to us for renewal!

The strength and weakness of such a week lay in the fact that it was hosted by a local church, instead of the more usual conference organised by a specialised team of experts. This meant that the quality of teaching on the part of seminar leaders was admittedly varied; but unless renewal could be seen to work within the context of an ordinary congregation – and we were a very ordinary congregation, with a complete mix of social and educational backgrounds – it had nothing much to say to the Church as a whole. Indeed, although the teaching and worship was generally appreciated, it was the impact of the church as a living fellowship, with all its obvious faults and failings, that almost always made the most impact. One church leader, who encouraged several other clergy to attend, wrote afterwards: 'I have seen all the people who attended the recent Renewal Week . . . They have all been blessed beyond words. One person put it beautifully: "It was a glimpse of heaven". This is precisely what our Lord means his living Body to be.' That, and countless similar letters, gave us enormous encouragement. From our perspective as elders, we often seemed to be limping from one crisis in the church to another. 'What next?' we often asked ourselves gloomily. We wondered if those who came to our church would have a glimpse of hell instead of one of heaven! But the Gospel always speaks of God's grace in the midst of human weakness, sin and frailty. There was no doubt about our weaknesses – one of our best Renewal Weeks came immediately after the traumatic closing of the Mustard Seed – but somehow God's grace was still there among us, which is why those who came continued to be blessed.

The leader of one of the many Irish contingents put it in this way:

The value of a course like this lies chiefly in the encouragement and stimulus it gives. People coming from local situations which seem fairly hopeless, can return home to weigh the biblical principles to see how they can be applied in their own churches. If God can do in such unpromising soil what he has manifestly done in 'redundant' churches in

York he can do new things in any place, if his people open up to him and in the power of the Holy Spirit respond where they are. This is the main message of the York Weeks of Local Church Renewal.

Another said, 'Here we *felt* God's love in action. He was really among us. We go back believing he goes with us.'

It was always a special privilege to pray with those who were longing for personal renewal. One older Norwegian pastor, who was also a gifted theologian, was so hungry to meet with God that he did not sleep at all during the night before he came to York. I have hardly ever met a man who was so 'hungry and thirsty for righteousness'. Naturally God met him with unusual power. We did not say anything very much to him. God did his own work, and it was wonderful to see it happen. We never quite knew why those weeks proved to be such a turning-point in the lives of many who came, not least clergy and ministers, but that is what happened time and again. At a recent leaders' conference for renewal in Wales, seventy out of the eighty leaders present had been to our Renewal Weeks.

It is important, however, to be sensitive to the momentum of the Spirit. When the wind of the Spirit seems to be blowing in a certain direction, we need the courage to hoist our sails and to move as the Spirit leads us. But when the wind changes direction, we need equal courage to change with it. In our churches, we must be willing not only to start some ventures we have never tried before, but also to stop them when their immediate purpose seems to have ended. Recently we noticed a slackening of momentum in the Renewal Weeks, and I am glad to hear that the present leaders of St. Michael's have had the courage to stop them – at least for the time being. Perhaps these weeks will start again at some later date, possibly in a different form. We need always to be open to the Spirit of God, who is the Spirit of movement.

Constantly we need renewal. The Holy Spirit will never let us stay in one place for too long, lest we become stale and stagnant. Always he is moving us on, to make us fresh and relevant for the needs of people today. We can never cling to what is relevant only for the people of yesterday – or if we do cling to those patterns we shall soon become spiritually sterile. 'He who has an ear, let him hear what the Spirit says (*lit.* is saying) to the churches.' The greatest hindrance to the work of the Spirit is not tradition, since tradition can have a vital stabilising effect in a confusing world of constant change, but *traditionalism*, or the clinging to tradition for tradition's sake. The history of the Church could be characterised by the breath of the Spirit of God breathing new life into the Church. Man then comes to regiment and institutionalise it; and the Spirit of God quietly withdraws. The institution, devoid of any real spiritual life, may continue to rumble on unperturbed, sometimes for generations. Occasionally I come across certain church events which perhaps were highly relevant at one time, but over which you now see written the word *ichabod* – 'the glory of the Lord has departed'. It is then that we need to cry out with the psalmist, 'Wilt thou not revive us again, that thy people may rejoice in thee' (Ps. 85:6).

18

Teams and Travelling

'Someone has told us that a bomb has been planted in the theatre. Will you get everyone out immediately!' I was leading the Merseyside Festival with a team I had taken with me from York. It was Youth Night, and the Empire Theatre in Liverpool had at least 2,000 young people in it. It was only ten minutes before the programme was due to begin when the bomb scare came. We asked everyone to leave as quickly and as quietly as possible, and within four minutes the theatre was empty.

The police cordoned off the area while the theatre was searched, and there was confusion in the streets. Someone found a suspicious package near the electrical wiring system, and so we were all ordered back to a safe distance while the Bomb Disposal Unit from the army was called. So we had 2,000 young people standing on the steps of St. George's, looking like a typical football crowd. Alan Godson, an enterprising vicar in Liverpool and a great personal friend of mine, persuaded the Fire Brigade to erect some lighting, and the team did some drama, interspersed with the singing of Christian songs and choruses by everyone. Alan then guided a police van to where we were standing, and Bishop David Sheppard and I climbed in. Bishop David led in prayer, and I preached – all from the police van, using their loud-hailer! It was the strangest pulpit I had ever used! After well over an hour, the suspicious object was found to be only a hoax, and we went back into the theatre to begin the Youth Night. 2,000 youngsters had gone onto the streets; but the impromptu

street theatre had been so effective that 2,500 youngsters
went back in for the main event, which went extraordinarily
well. In fact it was so successful that the following week, when
we had another Youth Night, the theatre was packed with
over 3,000, and more than 600 were turned away at the doors!
Many young people found Christ on both those occasions,
and we saw how marvellously God can turn any situation to
his glory.

This was one of the many unusual incidents in the work I
was now doing for much of the time. Six years before, in 1973,
five respected Christian leaders had written to me over the
course of a few months, and as far as I know they all wrote
independently. However, each letter said roughly the same
thing: 'I wonder if God might be calling you to lead city-wide
missions in the future?' I had for years been leading university
missions, but this was quite different. To begin with, I dismissed the idea without much thought. I knew that God had
blessed the big events of the past, such as the Billy Graham
Crusades at Harringay and Wembley in the mid-fifties. But I
felt sure that such events were not for Great Britain in the
seventies, even if they were still fruitful in other parts of the
world. The whole pattern of evangelism had changed, I
thought. Today, 'small is beautiful', and I had been impressed
by the value of the small evangelistic home meeting. It cost
nothing, required minimum organisation, genuinely reached
the 'outsider', and through such meetings many had been
brought to Christ. I was not interested in any more 'big
events'.

It was hard to ignore those five letters, however, especially
when I received invitations to lead united church missions in
Tonbridge, Bristol and Sheffield in 1974–5. I could not ignore
the possibility that God *might* be saying something to me
through all this, however unlikely it seemed to me at the time.
Tentatively I accepted the invitations, and was pleasantly
surprised when we had three thoroughly good missions. At
Sheffield, for example, 13,000 people attended the meetings
and at least 400 gave their lives to Christ. Further, Christians
came together from widely different traditions and de-

nominations, and undoubtedly there was some spiritual renewal both for individuals and churches. We soon changed the name of these events from missions to 'festivals'. I could see the value of the occasional celebration, especially with all the gloom, depression and hostility of today's world.

It is commonly said that Christians need three sizes of group for healthy growth into maturity – sociologists speak of this as of general importance for everyone. The Christian ideally needs the cell, the congregation and the celebration. The *cell* is the small house group, where there can be an intimate sharing of the faith. The *congregation* is what most Christians know about, when we come together each week for worship, teaching and the sacraments. But there is also value in the occasional *celebration* when we come together in much greater numbers but still as members of one family in order to worship God, to proclaim the Good News of Jesus Christ, and to encourage one another in our faith. Even in secular terms we all benefit from celebration: birthday parties, weddings, anniversaries, and so forth. The Royal Wedding in 1981 was a time of rejoicing for the whole country: everyone felt better for it. We need these special events to lift us out of the drabness of much of our daily lives, and to remind us of some of the good and positive values in today's negative society. So it is with the Christian family. It is easy to get engulfed by problems, personal or otherwise. But God's people are called to rejoice together in his presence, and to encourage others to do the same: 'O magnify the Lord with me, and let us exalt his name together!' (Ps. 34:3). In no way could these festivals ever replace the mission and evangelism of the local church. But if they could be used to encourage the local churches in their necessary and continuing work, they would be eminently worthwhile.

At Tonbridge, Bristol and Sheffield I worked with the Fisherfolk, a singing group gifted in leading people in worship. For several years I had been convinced of the value of setting the proclamation of the Gospel firmly in the context of joyful worship. In this 'feelings' generation I knew that most people needed to feel God's presence and sense his

reality before listening to his words. We found repeatedly in
York that those who came to Christ in our services were
initially aware of God's presence through the worship of his
people. It was then my task as a preacher to say, in effect,
'That which you have seen and heard I declare to you.' This
had been the method of Jesus and the apostles when people
realised that God was among them through healings or signs
and wonders. I knew that joyful and sensitive worship is a
wonderful way of opening people's hearts to the Spirit of
God.

As much as I enjoyed working with the Fisherfolk, however, I looked forward to the time when I could travel with my
own team. Slowly I built up a group of young people from St.
Michael's who were gifted in music, dance and drama – the
drama section initially filled by those who later became
Riding Lights.

Our first really major commitment came in response to an
invitation from the Bishop of Down and Dromore in Northern Ireland to lead a Campaign for Renewal in his Diocese in
1977. We went as a team of twelve and although inexperienced had a remarkably good time, especially during the
closing five days in St. Anne's Cathedral, Belfast. One strict
Calvinistic Presbyterian minister wrote to say,

> How my eyes were opened! What a new lease of life I am
> enjoying in Christ! It is almost like experiencing my rebirth
> once more. On the Sunday morning following your depar-
> ture I felt I had to be man enough to stand and let my people
> know that God had blessed me at your services with a
> baptism of his Spirit. Many told me afterwards that I did not
> have to tell them because they could see the difference.

Since then he has experienced deep fellowship with Roman
Catholic priests who have themselves been renewed – something unthinkable previously. Others spoke of our time in
Belfast as, in the words of one of them, 'the most spiritually
rewarding experience I have ever known'. All that was an
important confirmation that God was with us in this new

development, and we could see both clergy and laity come alive in the Spirit.

Once the basic vision of the work had been established and a regular full-time team had come together, the invitations to lead festivals came in (and increasingly do so) much faster than we could possibly manage. It soon became apparent that all these invitations needed careful researching. Which areas were ready for a festival? Were the Christians in that area beginning to work well together, especially the leaders? Did the proposed festival have the backing of the bishop and other denominational leaders? Was the Spirit causing a fresh hunger for God and a desire among Christians to make Christ known? Were we the right team for what was wanted? Obviously there are many different approaches, and ours may be one valid way of communicating the Gospel, but not the only one. It was clearly impossible for me to do the necessary research as the invitations grew in number. Providentially an elder in St. Michael's, Douglas Greenfield (who ran the Renewal Weeks) felt that God was calling him to help us in this, and, as consultant to an export pharmaceutical company, he was given flexibility of time to combine his business with this research. Douglas over the years has proved indispensable, and without his careful investigation and practical planning we would have wasted many thousands of pounds and endless time and energy in fruitless work.

The simple plan is for Douglas to follow up an invitation with a preliminary visit, in order to discuss plans with church leaders. He then submits a report, giving some indication whether a town or city is ready for a festival. If the report is favourable, we arrange a 24-hour visit for the whole team, leading a festival of praise in the evening and holding seminars the next morning – seminars usually on evangelism, small groups, music in worship, dance in worship and drama. By the end of that visit both the local church leaders and we as a team will have some idea whether a festival is right in the future. If we feel this to be so, much praying and planning begins.

When the festival arrives, the focal point is an evening celebration each night of the week, marked by joyful,

corporate worship and then preaching illustrated by drama or
mime. These are always festive occasions, even when we take
very serious and challenging themes. The rest of the time is
taken up with a wide variety of activities: visits to schools,
universities, colleges, prisons, hospitals; lunches for businessmen, seminars for clergy, special meetings for ladies, the
elderly or the sick; street theatre in shopping precincts,
children's services, workshops for local churches – anything
that is relevant in the area.

Our overall aim is threefold: reconciliation, renewal and
evangelism. As far as *reconciliation* is concerned, it is thrilling
to see Christians of all traditions come together, usually with
very few exceptions, and discover one another in Christ.
After an encouraging festival in Manchester in 1978, one
prominent leader in the City wrote: 'I have now been working
in the City for over twenty-eight years and I can honestly say
that there has never been anything like it . . . One of the
outstanding features has been the way in which so many
churches have worked together (250 of them), plus the note of
celebration and just a real joy in the Lord himself.' In
Birmingham (1981) over 600 churches committed themselves
to the festival, and once again there had never, in living
memory at least, been such co-operation between the churches. If new love and trust can be found within the Body of
Christ in a given area, that alone would make the festival well
worth all the time, money and effort involved. It is where
'brothers dwell together in unity' that the Lord 'commands his
blessing' (Ps. 133).

Obviously the theme of reconciliation is foremost in our
minds when leading festivals in Northern Ireland and South
Africa, and we make it clear in all our meetings that all
people, no matter what tradition, race or culture they belong
to, are welcome. Reconciliation, however, is never easy. In
Northern Ireland, for example, we have been openly opposed
by militant groups. In South Africa, one attempted city-wide
festival was frankly a disaster. One of our biggest disappointments, however, was in Malta. In January 1978 Douglas and I
spent a week in Malta at the invitation of several leaders in the

Roman Catholic Church to see if we should lead a mission for renewal in the island for Roman Catholics. Douglas knew Malta well through his business, and although I had an extremely heavy cold through the week, I found it a fascinating time. We had many sensitive discussions and we knew that it was remarkable that we, an English Anglican team, should be invited for such a purpose. On the last day, when everything looked set and all the plans were fully made, there was an objection from a totally unexpected non-Roman source. There was nothing that could be done but to call off the whole mission, and they (and we of course) were extremely sad about it.

Our second main concern is for *renewal* – that is, encouraging fresh spiritual life both for the individual Christian and for the local church. The advantage of a special week, such as a festival, is that it gives everyone the motivation for doing what should be done in the normal course of the church's life. Christians come together to pray; they learn how to talk to their friends about Christ, and start doing it; they meet for studying the faith; for worship; for projects in the area, both evangelistic and social. In fact such good work takes place before we arrive in a town or city for the festival itself that I am frequently told on the opening day, 'If you had died before the festival had started, it would all have been worth it!' It is a curiously ambiguous remark (since I had not died, was it worth it after all?), but I know what I hope they mean by such a remark, and am delighted that we become the excuse for so many good Christian initiatives in the area.

There can also be renewal in other ways. Many people find renewal in worship: 'For the first time in my life I am learning what it means to worship God,' wrote one person after a festival. Others discover a new confidence in God, a new understanding of the faith, a new assurance of God's forgiveness and love. One of the most frequent and significant results is the renewal of relationships. In the summer of 1978 we led a mission (as it was called) for the whole of Cornwall, based mainly on Truro Cathedral. The Dean of the cathedral, who was nearing retirement, said that in all his long ministry he had never sensed such a powerful presence of the Spirit of God as during those ten days in the cathedral. One night I urged all those present who felt that they needed to put right some relationships to do so before they went to bed, if possible. 'Talk when you get home,' I urged. 'Make a phone call; write a letter.' Outside the big west doors of the cathedral are many telephone boxes. I heard later that after the service was over there were queues of people waiting to make a telephone call, and I understand that many relationships were put right that evening. I did not know all this at the time. What I did know was that, in the cathedral the next night, the sense of God's presence was almost electric. The Spirit of God was no longer grieved through long-standing bad relationships, and was thus free to move in unusual power. This is an experience known to Christians throughout the world in times of revival.

In Ipswich (1981) the hunger for God throughout the whole area was so great that we could not deal adequately with the crowds that came. The Corn Exchange was booked for the main meetings, with overflows in the Town Hall nearby. But on the opening night some 600 had to be turned away, many of them having come in coach parties from some distance. The next night extra relays were provided, and the meeting was broadcast to a crowd of 200 standing in the cold, dark streets, with cups of coffee and tea being taken to them. Eventually the Christians had to say to one another, 'Don't come unless you have to!' Not many churches say that today. From Ipswich we went on to Northampton where we saw tremendous joy in God's presence as we came together from a variety of traditions. 'The gift of joy has almost overwhelmed us' is how one Anglican leader expressed it. We also visited Wellingborough Borstal when we were there. The prison chapel was packed with young lads, over fifty of whom committed their lives to Christ that morning. During the Leeds Festival (1977) we saw a particularly unusual healing. As the final hymn 'The Lord's my Shepherd' was being sung, a woman with multiple sclerosis realised that God was healing her. She got out of her wheelchair and, supported lightly by a member of my team, walked all round the Town Hall. In the course of a few months her healing became more complete, and she later married the Bishop of the New Hebrides, now the Bishop of Glasgow. These are only a few samples of the renewing work of the Spirit of God, and stories similar to these could be multiplied many times over.

My third and primary concern has always been *evangelism*. The reason why I travel with a team, gifted as they are in the performing arts, is that they are able to communicate the Gospel much more effectively than I could with mere words. It was in 1977 that we first went to Crumlin Road Prison in Belfast, and had two wonderful services for the prisoners, most of whom were terrorists. The Chaplain said to us before we went in, 'You will probably see more murderers in the next hour than in the rest of your life put together.' We were decidedly nervous, but found that the combination of drama, music and dance, and short simple preaching, created an instant rapport. When I led the prisoners in a prayer of commitment to Christ there was total prayerful silence. Many professed conversion that day, and the commander of one of the leading terrorist organisations wrote to tell me that he had been considering for some time becoming a Christian – which was an interesting point in itself. 'But,' he went on to say, 'after seeing your team I no longer had any doubts, and have now been saved by the blood of Christ.' Later he told his prison chaplain, 'For the first time in my life I feel free!' I have many such letters from prisoners, including a number of terrorists, and most of those letters comment specifically about the vitality and communication of the team, and also about the experience of feeling free once they had found Christ. In another prison in Canada, the prisoners wanted an 'encore', so we had to sing more songs, perform more sketches and even preach more of the Gospel. Once again many prisoners came to Christ in that prison, and as they were leaving one prisoner said, 'You have brought us much joy in this prison today.' Such remarks and letters are some of the most precious I have ever received from anyone.

I find that the team is effective almost anywhere, especially

with those who are right outside the Church. In 1978 we held a
festival in Newcastle-upon-Tyne, called 'Celebrate the
Faith'. It was an exciting week and the crowded City Hall each
night was filled with a sense of joy in God's presence. The
vicar and curate of an Anglican church in the city centre had
found it impossible to attract men to their church. It was a
rough working-class area, with only a few elderly women
attending the services. But the festival gave the two clergymen an opportunity to take lots of men they knew to the City
Hall. The men were thrilled with the sense of action: drama,
dancing, humour and vitality. It seemed like the atmosphere
of a football match, one of them reported. The result was that
a number of those men gave their lives to Christ, and the
whole work of that tough parish took on a new lease of life.

During that week in Newcastle we also held a service in
Durham Jail, one of Britain's maximum security prisons. We
were allowed to take with us into the prison various props for
drama, including a large step-ladder. It was a strange sight
seeing the team marching into the prison armed with a ladder!
Once again we had a most fruitful service in terms of prisoners
committing their lives to Christ.

We soon found that this threefold emphasis of reconciliation, renewal and evangelism is at the top of most church
leaders' agenda, and invitations to lead festivals became even
more numerous. In 1980 alone, for example, I went (nearly
always with the team) to Pasadena, Kansas, Vancouver,
Calgary, Edmonton, Saskatoon, Winnipeg, Bedford, Roch-
dale, Poole, Chelsea, Cambridge, Wellington, Dunedin,
Christchurch, Auckland, Brisbane, Launceston, Hobart,
Melbourne, Sydney, Armidale, Tamworth, Canberra, and
Sheffield. Almost all the places have vivid memories for me,
and always we were aware of God's presence with us, both in
times of blessing and in the moments of depression or exhaustion. Increasingly it was obvious that God was using the team
as a catalyst. A catalyst is nothing much in itself, but it either
precipitates change or speeds up what is already taking place.
We as a team know that there is very little we can do in a
major city during one short week. But frequently God has

used these festivals, superficial though they are at one level, to stimulate the work that is already happening in that area. If we did not see clear evidence for this, we would have stopped them a long time ago. The apparent glamour of jet-setting around the world disappears within a few days.

It is not easy sitting in cold and draughty cathedrals, waiting for the stage or sound equipment to be erected before rehearsals can start. It is not easy travelling from one place to another, so that when we wake up in the morning we sometimes have to think hard to remember which country we are in, let alone which town or city. It is not easy working in halls or churches where the facilities leave much to be desired. It is not easy living out of a suitcase for weeks on end. It is not easy sleeping, or trying to sleep, in strange beds for roughly half of each year. My particular trial is damp beds. I have endured these so often that I now automatically carry with me a 'survival kit for damp beds'. If I suspect that the bed is damp, I put a mirror between the sheets. If the mirror mists up, I am left in no doubt! I then put on a black nylon mackintosh, which I always carry with me, over my pyjamas, pull on thick socks and climb carefully into bed. It is not the last word in comfort, but infinitely preferable to lying in a damp bed when you get chilled to the bone and find sleep out of the question. In one vicarage where the bed was damp – vicarages are nearly always the worst, and I usually stay in vicarages! – I wore my mackintosh as usual. I was taken by surprise, however, when the vicar came in early in the morning with a cup of tea. I had to sit up in bed to take the tea, and I think he was taken a little by surprise when he saw me in my black nylon mac! A travelling ministry is not always easy; but it does have its humorous moments!

Above all, it is not easy having to say goodbye to my wife and children so often, and it is not easy being away for weeks on end. It is even more difficult for them. In order to retain some stability for our children Anne virtually never travels with me, and we have accepted the constant separations as necessary for the present time. We work hard to maintain communication, however. Anne and I write to each other about every other day, and I write to Fiona and Guy twice a week. I also telephone every day when in this country – once a week when overseas – and we try in various ways to encourage and support one another. Anne helps, for example, by seeing to a lot of correspondence in my absence, making decisions where necessary and, with my secretary, trying to avoid a mountain of demanding mail waiting for me on my return. Sometimes they hide the mail from me so that I cannot even see it until I have partially recovered from a tour.

After those ten gruelling weeks in Australia and New Zealand, however, I have resolved never to be away for more than five weeks at a time, if I can possibly help it, but even so the work places strains on us as a family. In spite of this, however, God's grace is there for every human need, and our family life today is richer than it has ever been before.

I have the privilege, of course, of travelling with a team, and the mutual support we receive is tremendous. All team members commit themselves for at least a year at a time, and I am always glad when some choose to stay longer. So many people have spent time with me over the last eight years that it is difficult to mention any names in particular. All have played a special part in the work, and indeed in my own personal life. Most important, perhaps, is not the individual performances of gifted people, but the sense of Christ's presence through our oneness in him. The depth of our relationships in Christ depends on the degree to which we are willing to share our lives openly with one another, and such openness brings pain as well as joy. For example, sometimes I battle with depression. I never know all the reasons for this 'dark pit', as it seems to me. Some of it may be hurt pride. Sometimes it is obviously exhaustion, physical, mental, emotional and spiritual. At times, when I am tired and strained, I can get angry over an incident that may be quite trivial in itself; and then I get angry with myself for getting angry. As I suppress both forms of anger, depression is the result. I am then even more difficult to live with than usual. I do not want people to get too near to me, but I hope very much that they will not go too far away either. My team members have always been extremely supportive when I have gone through these difficult times; and naturally others in the team have had their ups and downs as well. In this way, by our mutual caring the sense of our belonging together in Christ increases.

At the end of the day we know that we have nothing to offer anyone of ultimate importance apart from Christ himself. If he can be manifested more clearly in our lives through our conscious weakness, we are content to remain weak and vulnerable. I find both the travelling and the team work demanding in every way, but I am thankful to God for having drawn me into it against all my initial prejudices. I sometimes say that God sucked me in backwards into this work: I have neither wanted it, nor been ambitious for it. Fortunately God is able to use even reluctant servants to accomplish his sovereign will. I have also discovered, together with the team, a great sense of privilege and tremendous times of joy both in our fellowship with one another and in seeing God at work through us.

19

Move to London

July 26th, 1982 closed a major chapter in our lives and opened
a blank page. After seventeen years in one house in York we
moved to central London. The transition was not easy, and as
I write this six months later we are still suffering profound
bereavement. We knew that our relationships in York had
been deep – perhaps more so a few years ago than recently –
but we had little idea how deep they were until they were
severed. Next to literal bereavement within one's own family,
this must surely be one of the most traumatic events in one's
life. The sense of loss has been acute; and, as I have often
counselled those who are bereaved, we have to let time do its
own healing work. It is not that the Christians in London have
lacked in kindness and generosity. Far from it. We know that
we are a part of God's family wherever we go on the face of
this earth; and the sensitive caring of many Christians here
has encouraged us with God's love time and again. But deep
relationships are forged through suffering and pain, as much
as through joys and blessings. Without both warp and woof,
no tapestry is made.

'Joy and woe are woven fine' are the memorable words of
William Blake. God spoke to us through a close friend in
London that the riches we would find here would be 'the
treasures of darkness'. Richard Wurmbrand once said, 'The
most distant object you can see in the bright light of day is the
sun. But in the dark of night you can see stars which are
millions of times further away.' We shall doubtless discover
many of God's treasures through all our difficult experiences.

Outwardly we have not been suffering at all, but the inward grief has taken us by surprise, and that is why I mention it. Many thousands of others must experience the same pain of parting, especially where the relationships had been bonded together by the super-glue of God's love for many years.

'Why did you leave York at all?' is the question I am often asked, and it is not always easy giving the answer. I had always said that God called us to York in such a convincing way, despite all adverse circumstances, that it would require a spiritual bomb to get us out! It did not happen like that. Nor did we leave on account of the closing of the Mustard Seed or the split in the congregation. Indeed, while those problems were still around, nothing would have taken us from St. Michael's. It was only when the church had come together with a new unity and love, and when the Holy Spirit was manifestly blessing God's work there again, could we even contemplate the idea of departure.

The marriage ordinance in Genesis 2:24 is clear: 'Therefore a man leaves his father and his mother and cleaves to his wife, and they become one flesh.' Leaving always comes before cleaving. Now that our spiritual children had grown up into maturity, and were more than competent to take over the family business, it seemed that the time for leaving had come. No parents should hang around their children when they get married and start having a family of their own. Occasional visits are one thing; to live in the same house is quite another. We felt that the time had come for us as 'parents' to make room for others to take over, without us looking over their shoulders all the time to see how they were getting on. Apart from any other reason, it was primarily for the future health and growth of the congregation at St. Michael's that we knew we ought to move. The challenge for us of a major move at this stage would no doubt be good, even though we did not relish the thought of it.

Besides all that, there were other considerations. More of my time was taken up with travelling, including many trips overseas, and London was an obvious centre for this. Increasingly I received invitations also to consult with church leaders, and nearly all of these took place in the metropolis. I also needed more time for writing, and for preparing for the many speaking engagements I had throughout the year. As rector of St. Michael's I still had *some* parochial responsibilities, and crises were often awaiting my return from some overseas tour. Added to that, our children were at an age when a move was comparatively easy in terms of their educational progress; if we did not move now, it would have been much more difficult during the next five years. Cautiously, therefore, we responded to a tentative suggestion from one or two leaders to base ourselves in central London.

It was not a sudden decision; and I have to remember that when agonising doubts often assail me as to whether or not we did the right thing. Over the course of nine months or more, we spent much time in prayer and asked the advice of several discerning Christian leaders, from the Archbishop of York to friends in different parts of the world. Increasingly we heard the same conclusion, 'It makes sense.' One or two prophetic words, from those whose ministry I deeply respected, confirmed that God wanted us to be available for him to work in the wider Church.

So we moved. Undoubtedly it was a step of faith. Although the bishops seem right behind the work we are doing, there is no ready-made job with salary for the work I am doing, and I have therefore become a 'non-stipendiary clergyman' – which simply means that all my salary, house and expenses must come from 'other sources'. Housing in central London is not cheap, and I have the further responsibility of paying and housing a team of about nine others, although we have seen encouraging answers to prayer about this. In York our team had been undergirded by a Trust that had been formed through the generosity of one couple who, after being renewed in the Spirit, had given both money and property 'for the advancement of the Christian religion by the proclamation of the Gospel of Christ and the building up of his Body the Church'.

With our move to London, new Trustees were appointed to manage what was now to be known as The Belfrey Trust for our support and the team's. Even though we received a gift from the previous Trust in York, the budget was more than four times as great as anything we had known in the past, and therefore – together with many Christian organisations – we have to depend on the Lord month by month. Over the years I have never worried about money (perhaps partly because I never understand it!) and I always remember Hudson Taylor's principle that God's work done in God's ways will never lack God's supplies. If in the future we ever find ourselves in financial difficulties, it will be a clear sign that we need to re-examine the whole work very carefully indeed, since I have no desire to perpetuate beyond its usefulness what God seems to have raised up for the present time. He may well have quite different ideas in the future, although I expect we shall have some warning of this.

I sense that one reason for my freedom from parochial responsibilities is to concentrate more on writing. I have never considered myself a writer, which is probably obvious by this stage; but through the encouragement originally of Bishop Timothy Dudley-Smith and Gavin Reid, formerly of the Falcon Press, and more recently through the stimulating wisdom of Michael Green, Edward England (my literary agent) and Hodder and Stoughton, I have had several books published. Although the whole process is a nerve-racking business, I have been amazed repeatedly by the way God has used these publications to touch the lives of individuals and churches. One woman wrote to me saying that, after reading my book *In Search of God*, she knew that she must give her life to Christ. So she had a shower, dressed, did her hair, put on her make-up, and then knelt down by her bed to ask Christ into her life! She argued that, if she had an audience with the Queen, she would have done all that and more besides. So why not be presentable when meeting, for the first time, the King of kings and Lord of lords? It was fair logic, even though God would have received her just as she was, because of her repentant and believing heart. I do not know if any other of my books has ever had such an unusual response; but I do know – and for this I am profoundly grateful – that through them God has touched the lives of many thousands whom I shall never see this side of heaven.

One immediate joy in our move to London has been the creation of a new team. In York we had developed such close relationships in the various teams I worked with that I had been tempted to think it could never be the same again. For example, Phil and Joy Potter had been with me for four years and we had travelled round the world together – Phil as a gifted singer and worship leader and Joy as a dancer and constant encourager. When they both left to go to Trinity College, Bristol, to train for ordination in the Church of England, they left an obvious gap which I knew would be hard to fill. It was not easy recruiting a new team but we managed it, and in a remarkably short time we found that the Spirit of God was creating among us that same quality of shared relationships that I had known in the past. There is much talent in the present team – several of them have had professional training, and the quality of performance is good. But we all know that what finally counts is the reality of our life together in Christ.

We came together as comparative strangers at the end of August 1982, and our first festival was in Dartford two weeks later, based on the brand new Orchard Theatre. The festival went wonderfully well and we were all encouraged. That was followed almost immediately by a five-week tour in Montreal and Ontario, Canada, and again I was excited not only by the specific contributions of the team but also by our fellowship in Christ. Quickly the new team has learnt how to care for one another, pray for one another, worship God together and work well together. The quality of what we do off the stage determines the value of our ministry on the stage.

Opportunities for Christian ministry abound on every side. We continue to receive more invitations than we can possibly accept, and are currently investigating about thirty-five potential festivals both in this country and overseas, together with numerous other requests. London itself is also a vast and endless mission field. Many clergy and churches need encouragement and increasing renewal. Other churches have the potential to send out lay teams, some of whom could prepare the way for our forthcoming festivals, or else return for the purpose of follow-up. There is constant need for reconciliation, both within the Church and in the wider circles of society. Repeatedly I detect a growing hunger for God. There is no possible unemployment within the kingdom of God. In the words of John Wesley, we need to keep 'a cool head and a warm heart'. The prospects for the future are like the beginnings of spring – bursting with potential for new life.

As a family too we have had encouragements. Although the memories of all that we loved in York are still very fresh (at times disturbingly so) we thank God for the clear provision of a house which has a considerable measure of privacy about it – something which we find particularly helpful with all the demands of a public ministry. It has also been fun exploring new places together, from Battersea Park where I enjoy rowing on the lake with Guy, to Wimbledon Common, where Fiona rides and Anne exercises the dog.

Life is full of changes, some joyful, some painful. What is of inestimable comfort is to know that God himself never changes. His steadfast love endures for ever and his mercies are new every morning. These are the rock-like certainties we must hold on to when everything else may seem to be tumbling about our ears. There are many questions for us as yet unanswered. I do not know at present what my priorities should be, and where to give my limited time and energy. I am not clear which invitations to accept. All of us as a family have found the move much more difficult than we had imagined, and it is easy to dwell on the negatives. What we do know, however, amidst all our doubts and uncertainties, is that we cannot trust God too much.

Anne and I know that through the fires of past trials God has brought us into a much more complete marriage, and our family relationships are closer than they have ever been. God can use even our sins and mistakes, when surrendered to him, to increase the beauty of his pattern in our lives, and to make us more useful in serving others. Nothing is outside his sovereign control and constant love. He is the One who turns our negatives into positives, especially in the darkroom of suffering. That is the confidence we always can have when we pray 'Our Father, who art in heaven . . .'

Having written these words I heard only yesterday and unexpectedly, that I have to go into hospital in two days' time for a major abdominal operation which is expected to knock me out of action for the best part of six months. This has come as a total surprise, but I know that the matter is both serious and urgent. I cannot say that I have no fears but I do know that 'trusting God in every situation' is a reality and not mere words. Over the past few years I have been teaching large numbers of Christians all over the world the 'festal shout', based on Psalm 89:15, 'Blessed are the people who know the festal shout . . . For thou art the glory of their strength'. Over the centuries God's people have often been exhorted to shout praises to God, and the great liturgies of the Church have echoed these acclamations of faith such as 'The Lord is here – his Spirit is with us' or 'Christ has died, Christ has risen, Christ will come again'. These glorious words should not be mumbled, as is sometimes sadly the case, but shouted out with ringing confidence since, if we genuinely believe the truth of those words, they represent the greatest good news that we could ever know on this earth: whatever may happen, *the best is yet to be*! One particular festal shout that I have taught, which has rung through many cathedrals, city halls, theatres and in the open air, is the repeated acclamation in the psalms, '*The Lord Reigns!*' When once we gave this festal shout in Belfast Cathedral (on the day after a particularly horrifying bomb disaster in a crowded restaurant) you could almost see the faith of the large congregation rise above their fears and sorrows into a fresh confidence in the God who has the whole world, and therefore our own personal lives, entirely in his hands. That is the same festal shout with which I now encourage myself on the eve of my operation. I do not know what I shall experience nor what the prognosis will be, but I can rest in the marvellous certainty that the Lord reigns. Nothing is too great for his power, nothing is too small for his love.

Facing me, as I write this in my study, is a simple banner

made by Janet Lunt who was once a member of our household and who started the Banner Group some years ago in York. She, her husband Colin and their children, have all been very close to us. The banner I can see now consists of words in the shape of a tulip: 'TODAY my grace is sufficient for you.' God calls us to live one day at a time, each day trusting in the sufficiency of the Father's love.

One of my favourite songs is a fine one we often sang in York, since through the background of pain there is a ringing confidence in God himself. It is based on Psalm 16, and I quote part of it:

> For you are my God;
> You alone are my joy;
> Defend me, O Lord.
>
> You give wonderful brethren to me,
>   the faithful who dwell in your land,
> Those who choose alien gods
>   have chosen an alien band.
>
> You show me the path for my life;
>   in your presence is fulness of joy.
> To be at your right hand for ever
>   for me would be happiness always.
>
> For you are my God;
> You alone are my joy.
> Defend me, O Lord.[1]

David Watson

FEAR NO EVIL

Fear No Evil is a unique testimony of faith that will leave no one unmoved. David Watson tells with extraordinary courage and honesty of his year-long struggle with cancer: faith is tested to the limit, priorities turned upside down, but through it all a new reliance on God emerges together with the firm conviction that the best is yet to be.

'Poignant and radiant, matter-of-fact and sublime, modest and heroic, heart-rending and heart-warming in equal measure. I know no book better fitted to impart to twentieth-century Christians in the West the lost wisdom about death than this one. I am more thankful for it than I can say.'

James I. Packer

David Watson

DISCIPLESHIP

First mass-market edition. **'Block-busting'** –
J. I. Packer from his new foreword.

'Christians in the West,' claims David Watson, 'have
largely neglected what it means to be a disciple of Christ.
The vast majority of Western Christians are church-
members, pew-fillers, hymn-singers, sermon-tasters,
Bible-readers, even born-again believers or Spirit-filled
charismatics, but not true disciples of Jesus. If we were
willing to learn the meaning of true discipleship and
actually to become disciples, the Church in the West
would be transformed.

'The call to discipleship is a call to God's promised glory.
In view of the urgency of the times, we are to live lives
that honour Christ, that heal the wounds within his body,
and that hasten the coming of the day of God. This is not
a day in which to play religious games. Time is running
out fast.'

David Watson

I BELIEVE IN THE CHURCH

David Watson was known, loved and respected world-wide as a gifted teacher and Christian communicator. His dynamic ministry lives on through his writing and *I Believe in the Church* has become a classic. It draws on the years of leadership and learning at St Michael-le-Belfrey, York, to give a crucial message to the Church of the twentieth century.

David Watson

IS ANYONE THERE?

How can we find God?

'One half of us finds it difficult to believe in God,' writes
David Watson, 'but the other half is intrigued by the possibility that he really might exist. There is this unquestion-
able search for some kind of spiritual reality that will lift
us out of ourselves to what is real and true . . . Without
God, life is extraordinarily bleak.'

Is Anyone there? clearly sets out the facts about Jesus,
and how he is the way to God.